A Man of Many Dreams

A MAN OF MANY Dreams

An Autobiography in Poetry

Anthony Cardelli
& Cathy A. Cardelli Ciccia

A Man of Many Dreams
An Autobiography in Poetry

Copyright © 2014, 2015 By Anthony Cardelli & Catherine Ann Cardelli Ciccia.
Cover photo of the bridge taken by photographer
Rob Melone
Graphics, design and editing by
Catherine Ann Cardelli Ciccia

Never seen before photos of Frank Sinatra

All rights reserved. No part of this book may be used or reproduced by any means, graphic, electronic, or mechanical, including photocopying, recording, taping or by any information storage retrieval system without the written permission of the publisher except in the case of brief quotations embodied in critical articles and reviews.

iUniverse books may be ordered through booksellers or by contacting:

iUniverse
1663 Liberty Drive
Bloomington, IN 47403
www.iuniverse.com
1-800-Authors (1-800-288-4677)

Because of the dynamic nature of the Internet, any web addresses or links contained in this book may have changed since publication and may no longer be valid. The views expressed in this work are solely those of the author and do not necessarily reflect the views of the publisher, and the publisher hereby disclaims any responsibility for them.

Any people depicted in stock imagery provided by Thinkstock are models, and such images are being used for illustrative purposes only.
Certain stock imagery © Thinkstock.

ISBN: 978-1-4697-9822-6 (sc)
ISBN: 978-1-4697-9824-0 (hc)
ISBN: 978-1-4697-9823-3 (e)

Library of Congress Control Number: 2012909317

Printed in the United States of America

iUniverse rev. date: 01/12/2015

CREDITS

Voted Best Male Vocalist of 1991 by *The Courier Times*, Bucks County, Pennsylvania

The Courier Times: "A polished vocalist who is rapidly becoming one of the area's most popular night club performers. Cardelli sings in the style of commercial-pop vocalists such as Frank Sinatra, Tony Bennett and a host of others. His style is smooth and easy and the talented entertainer is as good as any singer in the Delaware Valley."

The Courier Times: "He's a smooth vocalist who sings in the style and tradition of his idol, Sinatra. But the talented entertainer does not live by Old Blue Eyes' music alone. His repertoire includes a hefty share of big band ditties."

The Courier-Post: "Cardelli doesn't attempt to imitate Sinatra's vocal timbre, but he does a fine job of capturing the humor, idiosyncratic phrasing and nonchalant sophistication of the Chairman of the Board."

Philadelphia Inquirer: "In a local café, they find a man crooning Sinatra from his heart . . . No, he didn't look like Old Blue Eyes. But if you closed your eyes for a second or two, you were fooled. He *sounded* like him . . . It's hard to believe, then, that Tony Cardelli has never taken a music lesson."

Posted in the *Trenton Times Best Bets/Best of the Weekend* entertainment edition in 1991.

DEDICATION

This book is dedicated to my daughter, Catherine Ann, "The Daughter of My People." Thank you for your great contribution to this book and all your hard work to see it published. It would not have been possible without you. You kept my sanity through the years, and I am so proud of you and grateful for the chance you gave me to see, before I leave, the added branches of our family tree!

CONTENTS

Foreword xxvii

Introduction xxxiii

MEMOIRS

The Way I Saw It around Old Blue Eyes 2

Tonsorial Artistry 14

A Beautiful Time 22

Trenton Makes, The World Takes 24

It's Not Over: A Memory from My Neighborhood 25

A Realization 27

The Gentle Giant My Uncle Joe Santarsiero An American Hero ... 29

He Can Make a Grown Man Cry: A Memory of Frank Sinatra 34

A Theory 34

"TT" 35

500 CLUB, Atlantic City, NJ 36

Anthony Martelloni An American Hero 45

The Summer Of 98' 46

To My Friends at Caesars Forum Lounge, Atlantic City,
New Jersey 2004 47

House Arrest 47

My Anna 49

My Grandson Anthony His Day in the Sun 51

Time Without a Length 53

Only Time Will Tell 53

Dear Anthony and Jillian 54

Living My Dream 56

Music To My Ears 56

Someone Once Said 56

My Love to Sing 58

MY MUSIC

My Music 61
A Song I'd Like to Sing 61
It Sure Feels Good 61
Under the Big Top 62
Same Old Song 62
I'm Not Ready 63

A TRIBUTE TO SINATRA AND HIS MUSIC

Although We Never Met 65
The Paramount 67
Bobby Socks 69
The Pied Piper's Serenade 71
A Rock-a-Dolly 73
Since One Million BC 76
Big Red Apple 78
Old Blue Eyes 80
Songs to Sing 80
Silent Beauty 81
My Swan Song 81
Old Blue Eyes Is Back 83
The Chairman of the Board 84
The Kid from Hoboken 84
To a Man I Never Met 86

MY DREAMS

My Dreams 88
A Fisherman's Dream 89
The Legend Lives On 89
Dreamers 90
I Don't Dream Like that Anymore 91
I Used to Dream 91
Night Nurse 92
Are You Just a Dream? 93
Now Is the Time 93
The Song from Our Dream 93
Let Me into Your Dream 94
My Favorite Dream 96

MY NEIGHBORHOOD

My Neighborhood 99
Where I Was Born 99
Two Silhouettes 103
Trenton 1939 103
The Midwife 104
My Song 105
The Twenties 105
Cabaret Show at the Kent Athletic Association Club 1960's 106
Characters From My Neighborhood 109
Diamond Jim 112
"A Warning to the Friday Night Out Boys":
The Battle of Who's Wearing the Pants 112
Richard Gizzi 113
Trenton Makes, the World Takes 114
Latitude Sailing Off the Jersey Shore 115
Diamonds in the Sand 117
From the Highlands Down to Ole Cape May 118
Go Fly a Kite 119

MY FATHER

He Built With His Hands 121
A Better Man Than Me 122
The Pope 122
My Old Man 123

MY SISTER

My Sister Went Away 126
Out of Place 126
Connie: My Sister Is on My Mind 127

MY LOVE AND ROMANCE

My Wife 129
In a Special Place 129
My Anna 130
My Pearl 131
She's a Diamond in the Rough 132
The Cosmos 132

The Sun, the Moon, and the Stars.................................... 133
Until 134
Alive 134
Is Yours, Is Mine 135
From the Day We Vowed 135
25th Anniversary... 136
Our Faith in Thee 137
Locked in My Heart.. 137
Beauty Is a Joy Forever 138
A Second Chance 139
The Moment 140
All My Defenses.. 140
A Winner Every Time 140
I Can't Get Next to Where You Are............................. 141
In Your Eyes.. 141
An Old ClichÉ.. 142
Blind Date 142
A Sight for Sore Eyes 143
Burning Up... 143
Don't Bother to Knock.. 144
Confession 144
The Only Way to Go 145
Even If... 145
Her Kind of Love.. 145
First Play... 146
Forever Yours 147
Forgiving You.. 147
Here's a Penny for Your Thoughts 148
How Do I Love Thee 149
Lady Luck... 149
Let's Make a Pitch 149
Ignorance Is Bliss 150
I'll Never Be Old Enough 150
The Woman in My Life 150
The Cross We Bear 151
Imagination 151
Our Music 151
In the Battle for Love 152

Right One for Me 153
The Only Way to Score..................................... 153
Love Is a no Score 154
Games... 154
A Good Time.. 155
Table for Two 155
It's Not Easy.. 156
Just a One-Night Stand.................................... 157
Just as I Predicted... 158
Just Like You Want 158
I Once Was Blind.. 159
Your Heart 160
Nothing.. 160
Our Gemini Hearts.. 161
Only for Your Eyes.. 162
The Two of Us 162
It Was Always Anna 163
It's Great to Be Alive 164
Gift of Time.. 165

LOST LOVE

Vows 168
A Home to Leave Behind.................................. 168
A House Full of Love 169
To Love, to Honor, & Obey................................ 170
All My Soul, My Heart 170
Behind the Smile.. 171
Some Other Bird.. 171
A Perfect Heart 172
Broken Heart 172
In the Darkroom of my Mind 173
Out of Sight, Out of Mind
(Is there such a place) 174
Four Seasons of Our Love 175
From Now On 176
Heart for Rent 177
I'm Running a Sale Today 177
All My Eggs 178

Never Falls on Me 179
On the Wings of a Dove 179
Time to Decide 179
A Long Time in Between Drinks 180
You Don't Have to Tell Me 181
I'll Forgive You 181
I Vowed 182
In Clear View 182
It Wouldn't Be Easy 183
Who Knows Better Than I 184
With Just One Word 185
Mood Indigo 186
Recapture the Rapture 187
You Don't Have to Tell Me 187
Sitting in a Bar 188
Collective Memories 188
Talking to Myself 189
The Love I Left Behind 189
The Memories of You 190
Two People 190
They Just Won't Go Away 190
Nice Guys Finish First 191
This Rainy Day 191
Time, the Tattletale 192
Traveling on a Metro Liner 193
Waiting for the Tide 194
Well Wishes of the Past 195
When I Lost Your Love 196
Where the Sun Never Shines 197
Whirlpool of Sadness 197
The Lost Love I Found 198
Sixth Sense 198
What Are You Looking At? 198
Without You 199
You Can Make It Happen 199
Me Without You 200
My Greatest Discovery 201

LETTERS TO ANNA
My Heart 203
Knowing Me 204
Just Before Sunrise 205
Being In This World with Me 206

MY DAUGHTER
I Met a Girl 208
She 208
Not Just Another Pretty Face 210
Class of the Fields 210
Elegance 211
I Was There When It Happened 212
Happy Tears 213
The Daughter of My People:
Our Family Tree 214
Just Once in My Life 215
From the Womb 216

MY GRANDCHILDREN
A Beautiful Story to Be Told: My Family Tree 218
Bursting with Pride: May 12, 1977 219
Wrapped in a Rainbow Towel 220
Beautiful in More Ways Than One 221
My Grandson 222
The Power of Beauty 223
Not for a Million 224
The Twelfth of May 225
A. J. 225
Chip Off the Old Block 225
"What's 'At" 226
I Couldn't Believe My Eyes 227
Raising a Boy 228
Elizabeth Ann: June 16, 1978 My Pair of Queens 230
Each Child Is Unique 231
My Grandson, My Granddaughter 231
Emotions 232

The Charm of a Newborn.. 232
More Beauty to Come.. 233
She Arrived: April 29, 1980 DeAnna Catherine 234
DeAnna 235
Grandchildren.. 236
Names.. 236
Carry On 236
Offsprings: The Beauty They Carry 237
A Note to My Grandson 239
Blow Your Own Smoke.. 240
Doctor Marin 241
For Elizabeth.. 242
Once Again... 243

MY FAMILY

Once in My Life 245
No Place Like Home.. 246
Long Way from Home.. 247
The Room that Warmed Your Soul 248
My Heart Skips a Beat 248
My Unlocked Heart 249
Feelings of Love 250
Love.. 251
Priceless... 251
Love Given to Me 251
My Eyes 252
Pleasure of Your Company 252
My Time with You 252
Without Limits... 253
Shallow Eyes 254
Since You Came 255
The Beginning of a Symphony.. 255
The Frameless Portrait 255
To the Infinitive 256
Triple Crown 256
When You Smile 257
We Had It All 257
Up Until Now... 258

Where My Heart Is 260
MY GREAT GRANDCHILDREN... 261

SEASONS
Christmas Mountain.. 265
Aquetong Road 266
Autumn Leaves 266
After the Trees Have Shed 266
A Welcome Scent in the Air 267
Crazy, Mixed-Up Day 267
CrosbyBlue skies smiling over a White Christmas 267
Close to Mother Nature 268
Four Seasons 268
Great to Be Alive... 269
It's a Miracle... 269
Mother Nature 270
Mother's Day 270
Spring... 271
One Spring Morning 271
Lullaby of Spring 272
You're the Reason 272
Spellbound.. 272

GOD'S LOVE
A Story Centuries Old 274
Before Man 275
From Seeds to a Rainbow... 275
God-Made Things 276
God's Gift to Me.. 276
God's Kind of Love 277
Old Father Time 279
On a Midsummer's Night 279
The Promised Land.. 279
Prayer... 280
Only Once in a Lifetime 280
Partners of Nature... 281
Standing on the Mound... 281
The Crack of Dawn 282

The Eyes of the World 282
This Side of Heaven 282
Somewhere This Side of Heaven 283
The Gift 283
Only God 283

LIFE

Life 285
Trilogy Road 285
Then, Now, and When 285
It Takes a Lifetime 286
A Hobo on the Rails 287
A Place with no Name 287
All I Ever Wanted 288
All Roads Lead to Rome 289
Business for Sale 289
Light on the Bet 289
Throwing in the Towel 290
Man 290
Two Candles 290
For Some People 291
Bending in the Wind 291
Don't Hold Back the Tears 292
From the Old School 293
I Told You So 293
The Other Guy 293
How Do You Know? 294
How 294
In Better Times 295
In the Prime of My Life 296
Is There Such a Place 297
Kick Out of Life 297
Two for the Price of One 298
Last Call 298
Merrily We Roll Along 299
Nightcap 300
Millions on the Run 300
Trees 301

Spinning 301
Time: The Tattletail of Life 301
Only Time Will Tell... 302
Poor Little Rich Girl 302
Sad and Happy People 303
Where Were You?.. 304
The Bitter Taste 305
Tough Love.. 305
The Courage of Billie Jean 306
The Eyes and Ears of the World 306
Thoroughbreds 307
What Friends Are For.. 308
The Second Chance on the First Impression 309
Women in My Life.. 309
When You Are Young.. 310
As You Grow Older... 310
The Essence of Life 311
Only Heaven Knows... 312
Another Lost Soul 312
The Secret of Living.. 313
Recipe for Happiness 313
Life's End 313

SELF-REFLECTING

All My Yesterdays.. 315
Without an Education 316
Among the Many Millions.. 316
As Long as a Lifetime.. 317
At This Stage of the Game 317
Between the Raindrops 318
It Might Have Been 318
Not the Garbo Type.. 319
Enough to Get By... 319
A No Vacancy Sign 319
Father Time 320
Forthcoming Seasons 321
Gemini 322
Half Past My Lifetime.. 323

In My Silence 324
Footprints I Lost in the Sand 324
Meeting with Myself 325
Positive Prints 325
My Bow 325
My Favorite Window 326
My Imagination 326
My Life's an Open Book 327
No More 328
Should Have 328
Been Here Once Before 329
The Star of My Faults 329
This Gemini 330
This Is the Last Time 331
Twins of a Gemini 331
Until 332
What's the Matter, Gemini 332
This Time Around 333
Myself and I 335
My Echo, My Shadow, and Me 335
Black e Blue 336

HOPE AND ENCOURAGEMENT

It's Half Past a Lifetime 338
A New Pair of Eyes 339
I Relish the Moment 339
Leave the Past Behind 339
Free as a Bird 340
Better Times Ahead 340
The New President 340
Don't Make Waves 341
Think of a Happy Time 341
Give It Your Best 341
Great to Be Alive 342
Keep Trying 342
First Impression 343
Heartbreak Affair 343
It's not Over 'Til It's Over 344

Let Yourself Go 345
Life Is Beautiful.. 345
My Special Star 346
Somewhere in Time 346
Now Is the Time 346
Illusions of Grandeur 347
She Opens My Eyes.. 347
Relish the Moment 348
Since Heaven Knows When 349
Sometimes the Sun Shines When It Rains 350
Thankful... 350
The Postman.. 351
What's the Matter, Friend? 352
With or Without the Sun.. 352
Where There's a Will.. 353
Life After Death 354
There Will Come a Time 355

FAREWELLS

A Heavy Toll 357
Before You Go.. 357
When I Die.. 358
Until the Day I Die.. 358
Dear Friends 359
Here's Looking at You 359
Rest His Soul 360
Take the Time.. 360
Tears 360
Touched in Time.. 361
Trail of Tears 361
With This Kiss 362
Eternal Love.. 362

EPILOGUE

A New World... 363
My Fourth String 364

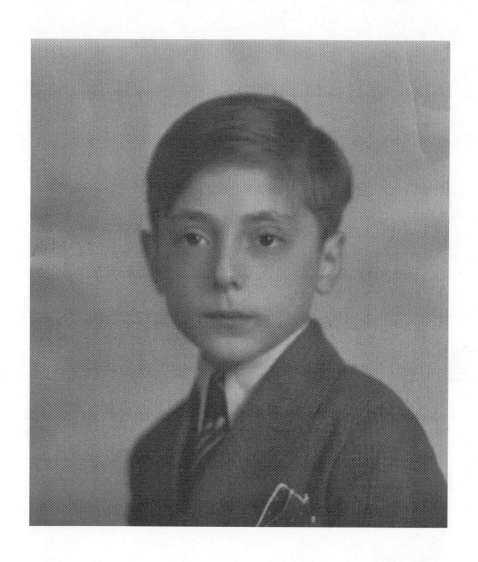

WEALTH IS IN DREAMS

I consider myself a very wealthy man.

A long time ago,

I was told by my best friend's son-in-law, Mr. Joseph Cummins,

that in Ireland, "A poor man is not a man without

wealth but a man without a dream."
I crossed an ocean, rivers and streams

before I married Anna, the girl of my dreams.

Together,

through the precious years,

we added the second, third, and fourth

generations to our family tree:

daughter Catherine Ann;

grandchildren Anthony, Elizabeth, and DeAnna;

and great-grandchildren

Gianna, Giuseppe, Marco, Annabella, Giuliana & Angelina.

I consider myself one of the luckiest guys

on the face of this earth.

Anthony (Anto) Cardelli

FOREWORD

One day not so long ago, my father selected four poems he had written years ago and asked me to send them out to be copyrighted for safekeeping. I did as he asked. Sometime after, he gave me one spiral notebook filled with more poetry and memoirs that he called his, "autobiography in poetry." He asked me to read it over and, "see if anything else in there is any good," to copyright for him. Well, from the moment I opened the very first page, I was captivated, amazed, and profoundly overwhelmed with emotions beyond anything I had ever experienced. I knew I had something very few children receive from their father. For me, everything he wrote was not only good but amazing. I realized what a treasure he had given me and that I had to preserve all of it, every word for my children, so they may know their grandfather more intimately and read about his life, especially his love for them. This is for my children most of all, so they will have their grandfather with them, speaking to them, for the rest of their lives. It is a part of him that will go on for all future generations of our family. It is a beautiful and special gift from him to his grandchildren and great-grandchildren.

I've always known he was writing over the years but was only familiar with a few things he wrote. I see now, after reading everything, that he would often quote from what he wrote. I remember while growing up I always thought of my father as a very deep person, a philosopher in his own right. I would often see him sitting and thinking. He would often refer to himself as a "Gemini": two people, always apologizing for the other guy. He still does to this day, saying, "I'm a Gemini!"

I couldn't believe how much there was and how beautifully he wrote. When he wrote about love, it was like hearing something from the book of Psalms, Song of David, or Song of Songs. Transcribing it all was not an easy task, and it took me over five years to complete. It seemed to go

Anthony Cardelli

on forever, because he kept bringing me more and more notebooks, week after week. The more I searched through his books, the more I found to transcribe. Only a few writings had titles on them, because he was just simply writing and writing. I gave most of them their titles from what I felt he would want to call them. It became an obsession with me to finish, my life's goal to complete it. It was so exciting for me to do this and such a special time in my life. I could not wait until I could pick it up again and continue reading and typing, but I was especially excited to finish it and present it to him and our family. As an effort to save time, most of them I read for the first time as I was typing them, and I would have to stop, sit back in my chair, and just cry out, "Wow!" I was filled with tears of mostly overwhelming joy. He opened his life to me through his writings and showed me so much more than the man I knew as my father. Yet, I understood and felt everything he was saying, because I did know him, for I am so much like him. It was as if I was hearing him speak to me with each one I read and typed. He was with me through it all: just him and I alone in our own world. It was especially emotional for me to read about his extraordinary love for my mother, who is now deceased, and for my children, his grandchildren. When I read what he wrote about them and his great-grandchildren, it fully explained the expression on his face when I see him look at them or speak of them. He has an extraordinary love for them, one that I have never seen in anyone before. He often tells me he cannot believe he lived to see each one of them, for it was another dream that was fulfilled. They are a part of his favorite dream that came true, his greatest joy, his very heart itself.

It was also wonderful to read about the times he lived in, growing up in his neighborhood of Chambersburg, the Italian section of Trenton, which he talks about often, and how he felt about God, nature, love, and just life itself. At times, it was difficult to read about the times in his life that were not so good. I believe he began writing during a difficult time in his life as a sort of therapy for him. Yet, he also wrote about history and the wonderful, joyous times of his life, when he was very happy. My father was a barber by trade, and he told me he would stay late at the barbershop, and that's where he did most of his writing. It was his way to express and release whatever he was feeling. As you read through his memoirs, you will realize that his passion for life, love, family, music and writing

A Man of Many Dreams

all began in the barbershop. Most of his poetry was written through the 1970's and 1980's and takes you on a personal journey through his life as it was happening. Because some of these writings were done years later, as they came to my father's mind, like those in his memoirs, there may be repetition between entries. I gathered all of the poetry by their subject matter and gave them their own chapter. They may also not follow in chronological order of when the events occurred.

My father was a barber most of his life, since the age of sixteen, known as "Hop the Barber," a nickname given to him for his love to jitterbug dance as a young man. I was told that all the girls would want to dance with him at all the local dances. Grown men still today tell me that my father gave them their first haircut. He often tells young people that you should have three strings tied to your bow, and that he did. He was a barber, entertainer and an employee of the state of New Jersey. Not only was he an artist as a barber and writer, but God has given him another gift to express himself: his voice. He is a exceptional and well known vocalist who performed throughout the tri-state area, including Caesars Atlantic City Casino Hotel. He is very popular and admired by everyone. Wherever he performed throughout his life, people would think that he was lip-synching because he sounded so much like Frank Sinatra. They could not believe it was him singing. He was not trying to sound like Sinatra: he just did. Ironically, he never thought he sounded like Sinatra and would always correct people and tell them he may phrase like him, but there was only one Sinatra and would always give him all the credit. It appeared so easy for him, so natural to sing. He captured the humor, idiosyncratic phrasing, and nonchalant sophistication of the "Chairman of the Board." He never took a music lesson, nor can he read music. What he did was listen to Sinatra from the age of ten. He would hang out with the bobby-soxers at the Paramount Theater in New York City from six o'clock in the morning to ten o'clock at night, just to watch each stage show Sinatra headlined. His passion for him has not dimmed with the years.

When my father sings, you can feel it's all from his heart. He simply enjoys it and loves what he is doing. He wants to keep Sinatra's music alive for future generations. It's when he is the happiest and doing what he loves best. Music is so much a part of him and who he is. When I was growing

xxix

Anthony Cardelli

up, there was always music playing throughout my house, coming from the barbershop connected to our home. My father is the reason for my great love of music, my love and passion to sing that is also so much a part of me. My father introduced me to The Great American Songbook, for which I have grown to love more and more each year of my life. To him, life is a song, and there is always a melody in his heart and soul. He recently told me there is always music in his head and told me what was playing just now. It is not surprising that he also writes so beautifully, as if the words he writes are lyrics to a song, his song.

My father is also a big fan of the movies and pretty much has seen them all, old and new. He can tell you who starred in them and can quote word for word most of the dialogue. The movie musicals and shows on Broadway are among some of his favorites. And not only can he tell you who starred in them but also who wrote the music and lyrics, who sang them in the movie, and who recorded the songs afterward. When speaking to him, he often refers to something said in a movie and relates it to your conversation. He really enjoys talking to people who have the same interest in the movies as he has.

Anyone I have met who knew my father always has such wonderful things to say about him. I never heard anything but great admiration for him—and not just for his singing. He is a very kind and generous man, and he is always a gentleman. He never has a bad word to say about anyone, and he has always been empathetic toward everyone's situation. He is a humble man and never gives credit to himself for anything: always to someone else. Just recently, my father and I were talking to someone we had not seen in a while, and this person said to me, "Take good care of this man. He's a legend!" Truer words were never spoken!

My father has always demonstrated how unconditionally he loved us and would do anything for us, and that he did. He has given my children and me everything he could, and now this! What a treasure and what a legacy he has left us. He is truly an artist, and he is my inspiration for life and the reason I helped him complete this book for our family. It was exciting when I was finished with this project, but a part of me was sad that it was over. I almost did not want to let it go because of the intimacy and personal nature of it, but I think it is just too beautiful not to share.

xxx

A Man of Many Dreams

I want everyone to see how wonderful, talented, and special my father is. I am very proud of him, and it has been an incredible journey to help him fulfill his dream to complete this book. It has also been the most rewarding time of my life.

And now, my father, family, and I invite you on this very personal and intimate journey into his life. And for those of you who know him, you will see another side to this Gemini, perhaps a side you have never before seen.

For a man with so many dreams, he never dreamed that what he was writing all those years would someday become a book. It is a fulfillment of his life and a more recent dream he never thought would come true. Until now! I hope you enjoy it!

Catherine Ann Cardelli Ciccia

INTRODUCTION

Music has always been the background of my life—ever since the day my mother, God rest her soul, asked Mr. Don Conti, a Trenton barber, if I could come after school and stay at his barbershop to wait for my sister, Connie, to come home from junior high school. I was only in the first grade! My school was two blocks from my home, and the barbershop was right across the street from my home. It was the Depression, and I had to obey my mother and father to help keep the pressure off of them, so they could go to work with a clear mind and know I was being taken care of.

The year was 1935. I was born in 1929, so I was six, going on seven years old. I came into this world when a lot of people were jumping from tall buildings. The stock market crashed, the country ran out of cash, and we were heading into the thirties with empty pockets and long bread lines. My sister, our first cousins and I were children at the time and somehow we never felt the Depression. My family made sure that we never would. In those days, you walked to school. There were no buses and no cafeteria. My mother gave me a house key. The key was known back then as a skeleton

Anthony Cardelli

key, long and black. Being in first grade, I came home for lunch. I would go to the corner grocery store and mark on the book, "five cents worth," go home all alone, and make my own lunch. I would make my baloney and mustard sandwich and a glass of Hershey's chocolate milk. Before I went back to school, I would pour "blue coal" in the kitchen stove, so it would burn until my sister came home. I also learned to check the flue on the stove. My father taught me this, and I was growing up fast.

The music on the barbershop radio was mostly Guy Lombardo, Glen Gray, the Dorsey Brothers, Harry James, and Count Basie. The barber loved Guy Lombardo and Paul Whiteman. Rather than just make me sit and wait for my sister for two hours, he made me a deal. For twenty-five cents a week, I swept the floor, cleaned the mirrors, wiped the tonic bottles, and folded the barber towels. Most kids my age were trading and buying baseball cards and playing after school, but I headed straight for the shop. I was learning to master the art of tonsorial artistry. I had a job at the age of six and developed a love of music that has lasted a lifetime. I was taping in my head everything that was said. Listening to answers of questions I could never ask at school or at home. I was on my own and by the time I was seven, I knew babies didn't come from heaven. The barbershop talk was putting me at least ten years ahead of my time. But my real love was music. An entertainer I wanted to be. The flame in my soul would light up and glow on the stars that I followed. All the stage, radio and movie stars all played a part of my favorite dream.

Although I never met Sinatra, I feel as though I knew him. For when I heard the first musical note from his lips, I knew it was the beginning of a beautiful musical friendship. The year was 1939 and the month was May. In fact, on the very last day, I became a year older than yesterday. He was twenty-four, and I had just turned ten. I became aware of being alive by the attention the whole world was giving to two men. Hitler was goose-stepping across the Rhine and Sinatra crossed the Hudson on a four-cent ferry ride. One wanted the whole apple; the other just a piece. I was keeping time to the beat of the Harry James Band, slapping a rag on every pair of shoes. I would shine giving my "All or Nothing at All" and "From the Bottom of My Heart," my best shot while working in the neighborhood barbershop. I was doing all the chores, along with picking up the tricks of the trade and collecting all the marbles in the game.

MEMOIRS

Anthony Cardelli

The Way I Saw It around Old Blue Eyes

In 1939, Hitler was goose-stepping all over Europe, while America was just starting to pick up the beat from the long, dragged-out Depression President Franklin Roosevelt vowed to defeat. I was ten years old and just about four feet small, but my mind was ten feet tall. I was working in a barbershop. In those days, if you wanted to know what was going on in the world and the little circle of gossip, the barbershop was the place to find out. I was taping in my head everything that was said. By the time I was seven, I knew babies didn't come from heaven. And Santa Claus . . . I still believed what my parents said about him was the truth. He was the only thing to hold onto to keep my youth. My boss was always listening to Guy Lombardo and the Metropolitan Opera on the radio, but I was trained on the sounds of Shaw, Miller, James, Basie, Ellington, and Jimmy Lunsford. And when I heard a vocalist who had just started with Harry James singing, "All or Nothing at All," I followed his pipes right down the line from the very first note.

Two years with Harry James flew by, and with all the money I earned, I piled up a stack of 78s, while the state of the nation was lend leasing to

A Man of Many Dreams

keep the peace in this side of heaven. But from all the shoptalk, I sensed at eleven this side of heaven was in for a surprise. And on December 7, 1941, all hell broke loose, when Tokyo flew from its coup to a place where all our carriers were in one group. On that day, most Americans learned a little geography: where Pearl Harbor was.

Everybody between the ages of seventeen to forty-five was taking the oath, raising their hand to make a stand. I was too young to go to war and too old to play kick the can, but I did my part in my own little way, printing signs of warning—"A slip of the lip will sink a ship"—and buying war bonds. But I was still buying records of my favorite vocalist, who, by the way, transferred to the Tommy Dorsey Band to replace Jack Lenard, who answered the call of the bugler. My man blended with Connie Haines and the Pied Pipers to tunes like "I'll Never Smile Again," "Last Call for Love," "Poor You," and a slew of others. I was making all the local hops, still working in the barbershop, when I thought my world was going to stop when he didn't want to get caught in the draft and went to join the big band over there. He took his physical in New York, and for the first time in his career, they turned him down. They found a leak in his eardrum.

It was 1943, and Tommy Dorsey set him free (the rumor was for forty thousand dollars) to make it on his own. I was fourteen and one inch under five feet. I was really moving up, chinning all the bars and downing coffee cups filled with booze to the old saying, "Bottoms up." I wore a "zoot suit" which was a one-button roll, blue shadow stripe suit with twenty-eight inches of material dropped over the knee, down to a fourteen-inch peg at the bottom of my featherweight, French-toed shoes. There was a hand-painted tie with its Windsor knot under a five-inch, roll-collared, white on white shirt, with a pocket full of silver and a solid gold chain twirling around my finger.

Still too young to go to war and too old to play kick the can, I was making the scene at the Steel Pier, a mile out to sea, cutting a rug with the rest of the jitterbugs to Woody Herman's "Wood Chopper's Ball." The man made a hit with Cole Porter's "Night and Day," the one number he did in the film *Reveille with Beverly*. I stood in line at the Paramount early in the morning to spend the day and night. Everybody brown-bagged it in those days. With one admission, we slept through the feature and were awakened by the screams of the bobby-soxers biting their nails and wagging their tongues. We knew the movie was done, and the man wearing a cardigan jacket and silk, oversized bow tie was going to pick us up on a high without booze and drugs.

The war was moving on, and while Martin Block was spinning the records for the home front with *Make Believe Ballroom Time*, a couple of DJs by the names of Tokyo Rose and Axis Sally were playing the hit tunes hot off the wax from Tin Pan Alley, spinning requests for uninvited guests—one from the East and one from the West. Never the twain shall meet, for after D Day, Hitler was running out of fuel, and the world he was burning backfired in his face. But we still had a long way to go. We still had Tokyo in the race.

A Man of Many Dreams

From 1943 to 1945, the man hit the beaches of Hollywood with *Higher and Higher*, singing songs by Jimmy McHugh and Harold Arlen: "I Couldn't Sleep a Wink Last Night," "A Lovely Way to Spend an Evening," "The Music Stopped," and "I Saw You First." He sang "You Belong in a Love Song" and was starring in *Step Lively*, singing Jule Styne and Sammy Cahn's, "Come Out, Come Out, Wherever You Are," "Some Other Time," and "As Long as There's Music."

In 1944, I was too young to go to war and too old to play kick the can. There I was, in my teens, between my dreams and reality. My past was a short subject, the present was an added attraction, and the future was a distraction about what decision to make, because there was a duration on everyone's life about whether or not they were going to be called to war between the ages of seventeen and forty-five.

That year, FDR won by a landslide and was in for four more years. I was fifteen, and since the age of three, he had been the only president for me. I left the shop I was working in for the past nine years for a raise in pay from five dollars to fifteen dollars a week, plus tips. Gene Krupa with Anita O'Day inspired me to take a trip with their hit record, "Let Me Off Uptown." I was heading in the right direction after nine years in a neighborhood shop. I made the move uptown, meeting people, not just faces. The word got around there was a "singing barber" in town. I was stepping lively, building a reputation with my scissors and comb, cutting D.A. (duck's ass) style haircuts without a clipper in my hand. But in my heart, I still was following the man. Then, in 1945, I skipped a day from school and went with a bunch of guys to see him at the Earl Theater in Philly. I was sitting in the balcony, and he was singing, "Violets for Your Furs." The room was in complete silence; you could hear a pin drop. Well, some wise guys dropped some pennies on stage, and he stopped the music. He picked them up and said, "A penny earned is a penny saved." He got a standing ovation, and those wise guys had to stand and hide in the crowd to throw off the slightest evidence they caused the thundering applause. I turned sixteen that spring, twixt love and war. It was another year to go before it was my turn to exchange my "zoot suit" for a pair of khakis, web belt, and combat boots. But on August 6, 1945 a new age was about to take place. Kids my age suddenly became alive at the cost of one hundred thousand people who didn't survive that dreadful day because of the splitting of the atoms dropped from the bomb bay doors of the *Enola Gay*.

I was sixteen, and time ran out for our nation's only thirteen-year president, FDR. It made me realize the only thing permanent was change. Truman took over the reins, and after "Anchors Aweigh," he gave the orders to drop the bomb on two cities not far from Tokyo Bay. Every town, large or small, had a ball on VJ Day. I missed being eligible to fight in the war by just one year. I had mixed emotions, but I stood up and cheered when Japan surrendered and signed the papers to make it official on the decks of the USS *Missouri*, with Old Glory proudly waving our boys back home to join the "52-20 Club" and take advantage of the GI Bill which meant that they would receive twenty dollars a week for fifty-two weeks. It was postwar year 1946. I was seventeen and old enough to take the state barber's exam. I passed it with flying colors in the month of June, and on July 6, 1946, I opened my own business, instead of going back to finish my senior year. Instead of taking classes, I stood behind the chair, cutting hair. I was a pioneer, who later would be called a dropout. The dark clouds of the war were in the past and left an over cast. But when I went to see my man in a movie called *Till the Clouds Roll By,* where he stood on a white kettle drum, dressed in a chalk-white, one-button, roll tux; white shirt; white bow tie; and white shoes, with fifty pieces surrounding him, singing the classic, "Old Man River," I felt clear skies were ahead.

Things were happening so fast. Industries made quick changes from bombs and bullets to cars with rubber tires. Synthetics were melted down, and there were no more ration stamps. You could have all the gas and cigarettes you wanted to burn, and plenty of sugar, coffee, and food. We were the victors, and we dwelled in the spoils, but I couldn't help thinking of all the people, our allies from Europe, who also won, going back to their bombed-out homes and so much work that had to be done before they could even start to get back what we always had. So, I would listen to the voice that always lightened any heavy thoughts that entered my mind. After *It Happened in Brooklyn,* the one movie he made in 1947, he was cast in *Miracle of the Bells* as a priest named Father Paul, to challenge the critics and show he could act as well as sing without musical accompaniment, singing "Forever Homeward" a cappella. In my barbershop, customers would rub me, as if I was going to go to church because I looked like a priest in my white, starched-collard, barber shirt with a black jacket. Little did they know I gave it some thought.

In 1948, I was making out like a bandit. I had already been in business for two years, and I was well established, with the shop open five days a week. I had Mondays off to give me time in the summer down in Atlantic City, New Jersey, to make my move when the crowd left on Sunday night. I had all the room and a lot to spare on the beach with all the "peaches," what we called the pretty girls on the beach. Monday was never blue for me.

If you think the ribbing in the shop was bad in 1947, well, this year, I was the laughing stock when my man came back with one called *The Kissing Bandit*. I was going to call Hollywood and ask them what were they doing with all that talent, but I stood my ground and defended him through *Take Me Out to the Ball Game* and *On the Town* in 1949.

Then came the year everyone wanted to throw back, 1950. We hit the half-century mark, and just seventeen days after ringing her in and less than five years after Japan's surrender was signed on her decks, the navy became a physical wreck when the USS *Missouri* ran aground in Chesapeake Bay. Douglas MacArthur was the man of the hour, and Margaret Truman's singing début went sour, while baseball's perfect mix of Joe DiMaggio, Yogi Berra, and Hank Bauer swept the "Whiz Kids" out of Manhattan Towers. On Broadway, Mary Martin was washing that man right out of her hair under an open shower in *South Pacific*.

Ezzard Charles stopped Joe Louis, the "Brown Bomber," who came back to pay Uncle Sam, the same "man" he gave up all his earnings to during the war and didn't keep score, but made the mistake to tax himself a dollar or two. The swinger of the year wasn't Ted Williams but a portly king named Farouk. He stripped his mother, Queen Nazli, clean—crown and all. If there were an Oscar for "People with Family Problems" he would have won. After examining him, the whole world could take heart.

A Man of Many Dreams

1945-1950 At Seaside Heights,
NJ Front Row Left: Dominick Argenti "Crow" & Myself
Back Row Left: Andrew Iavarone "Squarehead" & Thomas Argenti "TT"

Things were dull as usual in the White House. The eightieth Congress declared a two-month recess in September so members could go home and campaign for elections. Most people agreed with Truman's appraisal of the Eighty Worst leaving Washington, with Joe McCarthy, Alger Hiss, and Whittaker Chambers still digging up the pumpkin papers down on the farm somewhere in Maryland, with spies and bombs and the secrets thereof. The Rosenbergs—Julius and Ethel—were convicted in a controversial trial. Prices were rising, along with Mount Everest, the world's tallest challenge. An earthquake raised her peak 198 feet.

Sinatra, Bob Hope & Bing Crosby

The year 1950 was the year that launched the cashless society. Thanks to a man by the name of Francis Xavier McNamara and the Diners Club, for the sum of five dollars, you would have top priority at twenty-seven New York restaurants. You could stay over at two hotels and have all you wanted to eat and drink with just a stroke of a pen. "Dine N Sign" was the famous line. The joke of the cold war crowd was how we could go to war with Russia, a country that accepted our Diners Club card.

While all this was going on, my man didn't make a movie, and club dates were declining. His concentration was divided, and I felt he was undecided on what decisions to make. I was twenty-one, and the way this was going, I knew before I was twenty-two my draft card would be due. Sure enough, by the end of the year, army doctors were looking up my nose and sticking things in my ears. I took the smear, cleared my throat, raised my right hand, took the oath, and for the next two years, reluctantly joined the rest of the guys like me who missed World War II. It wasn't so bad at first: meeting new faces through "basic," weeding out the stiffs, and mixing with the willows, who bended backward to be a friend.

A Man of Many Dreams

Three square meals a day, with Uncle Sam footing the bill on a cruise across the Pacific. But a lot of guys failed him with their guts blown to bits on Pork Chop Hill. While over there, I kept in touch with what I loved best: my music. Jo Stafford was back in style with her hit, "You Belong to Me" and Joni James, a newcomer in the game, came up with a question, "Why Don't You Believe Me?" The man who was on a break came back for old time's sake, with Harry James backing his stock with, "Castle Rock."

I was with the 366th EAB., on an airstrip about thirty miles from Pusan. We were nicknamed SCARWAF (Special Category of Army Regulars with Air Force). Our job was patching potholes for the fly boys, landing on the soles of outdated bombers. We were housed in tents along the airstrip. I was a switchboard operator, along with six other guys to break up the twenty-four hours in the day. I was on duty on the board for six hours followed by thirty-six hours off. That gave me plenty of time to cut hair in the dayroom, where they set up a shop for me. The barber trade let me meet fellows from all over the base. While cutting their hair, I used to sing all the songs my man recorded, and once in a while, I'd do a few others, just to prove I knew there were other singers in the business. The service for me wasn't a hardship. I made the best of it, and with the gift of my hands and the fact I'd been working since I was six, I knew this too shall pass. And pass it did; I was on my way home in February of '53, stopping in Japan to pick up the ship that was going to take me through the Golden Gate, but this time *to* Frisco, not away from it. I was invited to the NCO Club in Itasuki and got up and sang with an eighteen-piece orchestra that played stock arrangements of big bands from the States.

In 1959, Eisenhower was running out of power. We were ready to follow the path, with Kennedy leading us to a "New Frontier," which could end in an atomic explosion. It would split people like the Adams, the Smiths, the Cohens, and the Kellys. It would split the rainbow of its colors. People were digging bomb shelters and bringing out everything they kept hidden in their cellars.

Korea 1952

Korea 1952—With my Cousin Albert Valli

Tonsorial Artistry

1944 Outside Brownie's Barbershop, downtown Trenton, NJ with "Dimples"

Anthony Cardelli

TONSORIAL ARTISTRY

I went into a barbershop across from my home after schools from Monday through Friday. It was 1935 and I was six years old. I was in the first grade. The barber, Mr. Don Conti, and my mother arranged it so I wouldn't be a keyless little boy, waiting for my sister, who was in first-year middle school. The barber gave me chores, like shining shoes, sweeping the floor, keeping the mirrors clean, cleaning the sink, folding towels on the mirror case to shapes of skyscrapers, and running out for cigarettes. There were no machines available; you could buy them loose, two for a penny. What an era to live in. You could buy cigarettes over the counter with just pennies.

For this, he paid me twenty-five cents a week. Well, think about it: a six-year-old boy working in a men's barbershop. By the time I was seven, I knew babes didn't come from heaven. Naturally, my priorities changed. I couldn't wait for the bell to ring at 2:30 p.m. I ran the three blocks from school to the shop. I listened to conversations from all classes of people: tradesmen, doctors, lawyers; everybody got a haircut—even the president of the United States. In fact, a barber was the closest person with a scissors and razor to the president. Haircuts were thirty-five cents, and a shave was fifteen cents. That's why the slogan, "Shave and a hair cut, two bits," became popular in the early twentieth century. The slogan went something like this: "Shave e a haircut two bits, who you gonna marry, Tom Nix?" Tom Nix was a famous cowboy back then.

My first cousin Louie was Don's helper. He did most of the shaves. The start of World War II lifted the Depression, and jobs were on the rise. The economy skyrocketed, and with the change and a sudden disagreement between my cousin and Don, my cousin left for a higher-paying job in the munitions factory. General Motors changed to making airplane parts and producing military autos for the war. No civilian cars were made until after the war.

When I was only twelve years old, Don told me to wash my hands and lather up the next customer for a shave and massage. Now, all of a sudden, I was going to do something different than what I had been doing for the past six years. During those years, I had watched how he operated. He was

14

like a father to me at the time. Don was teaching me how to have a sharp edge on the razors he needed to give a smooth shave. Stretch 'n' Stroke—I was learning the fine points of tonsorial artistry. He offered me five dollars a week. I thought it was a generous offer. To practice, I was shaving labels off of empty bottles not to leave an impression on the bottle and shaving soap off the balloons; if it broke, your hand was too heavy. I was twelve years old when I passed the shaving test. I was allowed to cut my friends' hair on a Sunday. Don gave me a key to his shop at just twelve years old.

I was setting up the customer, but the chair was too high. The liner was head high, so I got my shoeshine box and placed it at the foot of the chair. I stepped up on it—one step for chance, the other for luck—and started my apprenticeship of tonsorial artistry. I apprenticed from 1937 until 1944 in Don's Barbershop. Seven years plus two: nine years of my life. Still too young to go to war and too old to play kick the can, I took my precious memories with me, I started in Brownie's Barbershop after school. I was excited, because I was just starting first year high in public school, and the shop was "uptown." Brand-new school, brand new job!

1944 Outside Brownie's Barber Shop, downtown Trenton, NJ with Tut Petrano on my right

HOP'S BARBER SHOP
Roebling Avenue, Trenton, NJ

1960's Hop's Barber Shop on Roebling Avenue, Trenton, NJ

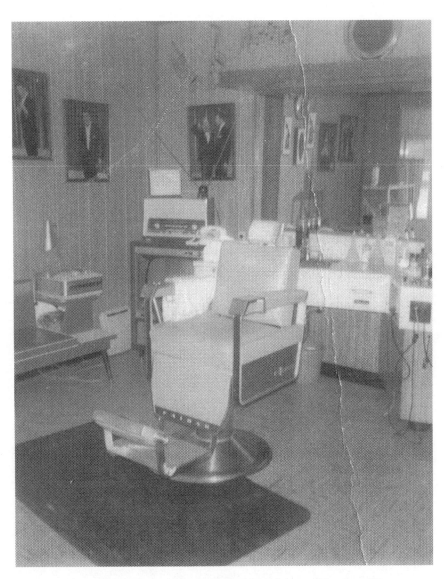

1960's Hop's Barber Shop on Roebling Avenue, Trenton, NJ

1958 Hop's Barber Shop on Roebling Avenue, Trenton, NJ and my daughter Catherine

1958 Hop's Barber Shop on Roebling Avenue, Trenton, NJ
and my daughter Catherine

1970's Heads You Win Hair Salon on South Broad Street, Trenton, NJ

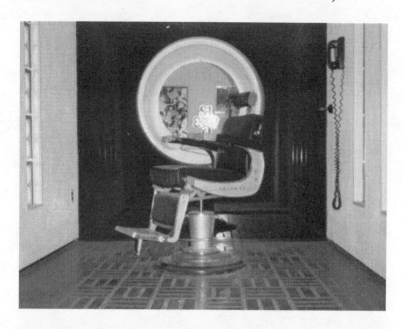

First Holy Communion 1936

A Beautiful Time

The snow covered the ground and trees. It was a beautiful time and one that I will always remember, along with happy tears.

Growing up during the Depression would remind me in my later years that if you don't expect anything (material things), you'll never be disappointed. During the Depression, from 1929 to 1939, money was scarce. The richness was food. As long as your belly was full, you were rich. A hundred pennies and you were a millionaire. You could buy over twenty dollars' worth of food compared to the prices today. Cold cuts were a nickel a pound; cigarettes were ten cents a pack. A full-course meal—including a cocktail, a mug of beer, dessert, and coffee—at the best restaurants totaled a dollar and twenty-five cents. The theaters were five or ten cents for first-run movies. White-collar workers averaged fifteen to twenty dollars a week. Masons, electricians, etc., earned three to five dollars a day. The moneymakers were in the rackets: number writers, bookies, and whatnot. Kids under ten years old earned their money shining shoes.

On Anderson Street, Trenton, NJ with my mother
Maria Antonia Santarsiero Cardelli

When I was ten years old, in the year of '39, I was beginning to become aware of the surroundings that encircled my home: grocery stores, tailor shops, shoemakers, bars, Model Ts, barbershops, restaurants, and candy stores. You didn't have to go out of bounds. Everything you wanted was all around you. The name of our street was Swan Street; it was paved with yellow bricks. In the two-block area, there was the Agabiti Construction Company, Don's Barbershop, the Agabiti Social Club, and a row of car garages for the Coca Cola trucks. There was also a blacksmith barn, which was painted red; he had a big, black, Italian bulldog that loved children. I can't remember his real name, but we called him "Lazy Bull," because he would lie out in the middle of the block all day long. He looked mean, but his bark was a front.

The row houses were on my side of the block: five houses attached to the right and an apartment and house with a candy store front, which faced Chestnut Avenue. To the right was Brown Trucking Company, and the rest of the block was the Coca Cola Company and garages for their trucks. The second part of Swan Street was intersected by Whittaker Avenue. The ice house took most of the right side, and on the corner of Swan and Hudson Street was my father's church: the Swan Café. No one had refrigeration, so the Ice House did a tremendous business. I would go with the family wagon and get a ten-cent chunk of ice to put in our upright cooler, which was called the icebox. Everybody spoke the native tongue. The sound was clearly understood. Today, it's called a ghetto; way back then, it was my neighborhood.

1944 Outside our home on Swan Street, Trenton, NJ with my mother my father Biagio and my sister Connie (Concetta)

Anthony Cardelli

Trenton Makes, The World Takes

"Trenton Makes, the World Takes": the capital city of the Garden State. She's been in business since 1679, one hundred years before the Father of our Country decided it was time to cross the Delaware and break through enemy lines to catch the British napping in celebration. With all his might, George Washington put up a hell of a fight to sleep in Trenton one night. The battle was won, and the turning point made way for the freedom all Americans cherish today. With three hundred years in her history books, Trenton began its decline in the late sixties. But I have confidence in the people to give her a facelift and restore the look that colonial man and woman fought so hard to keep.

I love Trenton; it's my roots! I was born here from parents who came from another land. I'm not three hundred years old, but many times I would walk along the banks of the Delaware and transcend in time through my imagination and feel the closeness of colonial man who once walked on the same piece of land.

A Man of Many Dreams

IT'S NOT OVER:
A MEMORY FROM MY NEIGHBORHOOD

It's not over. The shouting and the roar of the crowd will forever ring in my ear, and the smell of the greasepaint will forever flow through the air I breathe. I followed entertainers from the Broadway stage, silver screen, radio, etc., for they all played a part of my favorite dream: to be on their team. I was a year away from life in my teens. The year was 1941, and before the year came to an end, on a Sunday afternoon, at about one o'clock, radio programs were interrupted with news Japan had awakened America with bombs over Pearl Harbor. The United States declared war on Japan and the Axis, and World War II began for us; the United States was the missing link to make World War II official.

Almost overnight, all the industries converted to making war materials. The 1942 auto industry produced warplanes and tanks instead of civilian cars. Men between the ages of seventeen and forty-five were drafted. Women wore long pants. (The word "slacks" came later.) They replaced men who left to defend our country and the world. The factories never shut down. There were three shifts around the clock. Bars never closed to accommodate the workers. New York, the "city that never sleeps," was joined by the world that never slept. I was thirteen and still learning the barber trade. On Sundays, our mothers sent us uptown to invite soldiers who were stationed or being processed for overseas duty for pasta and meatballs at our homes in Chambersburg, the Italian ghetto. Chambersburg was like Little Italy. Also on the other side of the 'burg were the Polish and Hungarians, etc. All the English and Irish moved out when we moved in. The only Irish and English we saw were the cops and politicians. We were called the "G" word and the "W" word.

1936 Aunt Millie's House: Cousins, Santina Nicolai, Catherine Telesca (Kay), Aunt Millie(Carmela), Myself, Columbrina Nicolai & Felix (Phillip) Melleno

1941 On Chestnut Avenue, Trenton, NJ Left: Cousin Santina, Grandmom Maria Giuseppa Claps Santarsiero, Myself & my sister Connie

A Realization

It was June 1952, in the middle of the Pacific, en route to South Korea. The ocean was calm, and no one openly objected or burned their draft cards. It wasn't our time to; we were leftover patriots from World War II. It was strange to see the enemy, going about their daily routine like any other human being all over the world. We were twenty-two years old and had missed World War II because of our age. In 1941 through 1945, we were eleven to sixteen years old. We were taught that the Japanese were a vicious and violent race. Hollywood made films that showed they had no mercy for our boys. When I was there among the civilians, seeing that they were just like everybody else was confusing for me. My hate for them soon left, and I realized that they were not to blame.

The Gentle Giant
My Uncle Joe Santarsiero An American Hero

Uncle Joe, Myself & Pop

A Man of Many Dreams

The Gentle Giant
My Uncle Joe Santarsiero An American Hero

I owe my gratitude to my Uncle Joe for being born in this country. My Uncle Joe (Giuseppe Santarsiero) was a quiet, gentle little guy with a heart of a giant. He came to America on his own. He wanted to see what he dreamed of when he set foot on the docks of Ellis Island in the year 1906. Everything he saw was what he dreamed. He went back to Italy and told my grandfather he wanted to take his five sisters and my grandmother to America. My grandfather wanted to live his life out where he was born. My uncle told him that if you don't want to come, my five sisters and I are going without you. It was not until several years later that my grandfather agreed.

My grandfather Nicola Santarsiero and my grandmother Maria Giuseppa Claps along with their seven children who included my mother Maria Antonia and my Uncle Giuseppe (Joe) left their small village named Sant'Ilario which was in the city of Avigliano, province of Potenza in the region of Basilicata, Italia. They boarded on the ship Ancona from Naples, Italy on November 8, 1913 and arrived on Ellis Island, New York City on November 21, 1913. They rented a row house in 1914 on Anderson Street in Trenton, New Jersey. My uncle opened up a candy cigar store a few blocks away from where my family lived. He also had a back room which the men would play cards and win chips to buy a stogy and a cup of Italian coffee mixed with anisette. During the 25 years my uncle owned the store, his customers only knew him as a quiet little man. Few were aware that this timid soul turned tiger one night many years ago.

In the year 1914 it was the beginning of the First World War America stayed out of, until 1917. My Uncle Joe was at the age to be drafted. The American Army wanted to transfer him to the Italian Army. It was the practice in those days to assign Italian-Americans to fight with the Italian troops who were our allies in that war. They would still be American soldiers, but, the U.S. Army thought they would be more effective fighting with the Italian Army. My uncle refused and wanted no part of that scheme. He told them "No sir, I will not fight in the Italian Army. I came to this country because I love the United States. If

Anthony Cardelli

I am going to fight, and perhaps die, I want to die for the United States. He was assigned to Company M. 311 Inf., 78th Division and shipped to France. He and his buddies were pinned in their foxhole one night. A German machine-gun nest was inflicting heavy losses on the American troops. My uncle determined the location of the deadly machine-gun from the muzzle flashes. He crawled along the ground, under fire, until he was in range to hurl a grenade. In the darkness he hit a tree and the grenade bounced back at him. Quickly he recovered it and hurled it again, this time with devastating accuracy. He killed the German soldiers and silenced their weapon. Then he noticed a wooden shack about 20 yards away from the machine-gun nest. He started toward it, but, instinct told him to use caution. He lobbed another grenade which exploded on the roof of the shack. Within seconds six German officers came running out, my Uncle Joe ordered them to drop their weapons. Then he marched his prisoners back to his cheering buddies who hoisted him on their shoulders and carried him in a parade of triumph around the company area. You wonder what makes a man just rise up and face death. I found out the answer one day when I was reading from a book in my local library. The author was an American philosopher and poet, Ralph Waldo Emerson. He said, "Heroism feels and never reasons and therefore is always right."

My grandmother was home alone when the army officials knocked on her door one day to give her the news that her son was a hero. When she opened the door and saw them standing there she thought that her son was killed in action. She didn't speak English and did not understand what they were saying to her. She broke down that day and did not know what had occurred until some time later. I can still see her sitting in her favorite black rocking chair that a carpenter friend of the family made for her. I loved how she pronounced my first name. I can still hear her voice calling me, An-da-nee, An-da-nee.

For his heroic action, and for saving the lives of his buddies, he was nominated for the Congressional Medal of Honor by his superiors, but, received the Distinguished Service Cross instead, the nation's second highest military honor. A good friend of my uncle tried some years later to convince him to appeal that decision to the U.S Defense Department Decorations Board so he could finally receive the nation's highest military honor. My uncle refused because he was too modest a man to question an official's decision. He did not want any awards. He told his friend that he has his reward by living in this country which he loved so much.

He left a legacy of love behind him. Love for his family and a never ending love of his country, his adopted country.

1st Row: Uncle Joe (Giuseppe), Grandmom Maria Giuseppa Claps & Aunt Jennie (Vita Crecenzia) 2nd Row: My mother's twin sister Aunt Millie (Carmela Maria), Mom (Maria Antonia), Aunt Marie (Donata Maria), Aunt Margaret (Margherita) & Aunt Angelina (Angela Maria)

Passport Papers of the Santarsiero Family Coming to America on the SS Ancona, November 8, 1914

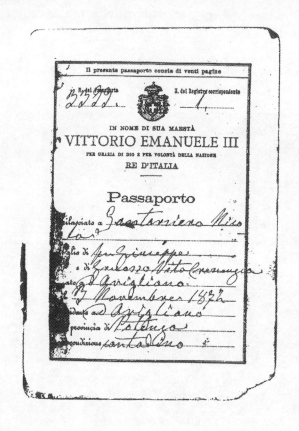

— 2 —

Connotati del Titolare del Passaporto

Statura m. _giusta_

Età _anni 31_

Fronte _regolare_

Occhi _castani_

Naso _grossetto_

Bocca _giusta_

Capelli _castani_

Barba _rasa_

Baffi _castani_

Colorito _bruno_

Corporatura _giusta_

Segni particolari _rpatriesoto_
rimento

FIRMA DEL TITOLARE

2796

— 3 —

Il presente passaporto è rilasciato per (1) _Neu York_
Santarsiero Nicola fu
Giuseppe
ed è valido (2) _per tre anni_

(3)

RILASCIATO GRATUITAMENTE A NORMA

DELL'ARTICOLO 6, COMMA 4°, DEL RE

DECRETO 31 GENNAIO 1901, N. 36.

POTENZA _7 Ottobre 19_____

IL PREFETTO

(3) Luogo per l'apposizione della marca speciale (o per la dichiarazione che il passaporto viene rilasciato gratuitamente a norma dell'art. 6, comma 4°, del regio decreto 31 gennaio 1901), bollo, data e firma dell'autorità che rilascia il passaporto Se si tratta di passaporto rilasciato all'estero, in sostituzione della marca speciale l'ufficiale che lo rilascia annotera accanto al bollo, l'ammontare della tassa percetta.

+ 81914

— 4 —　Persone che accompagnano il Titolare　— 5 —　(Art. 4 del R. Decreto 31 gennaio 1901).

COGNOME E NOME	Rapporto col Titolare	ETÀ	Luogo di nascita	Osservazioni
1 Ulap maria Giuseppa	moglie	nata 31-1 1874	Arigliano	W
2 Santarsiero Giuseppe di Nicola	figlio	nato 18-2 1896	Arigliano	
3 Santarsiero Vitascienza di Nicola	figlia	nata 19-1 1849	Arigliano	
4 Santarsiero Maria Anna di Nicola	figlia	nata 25-5 1902	Arigliano	
5 Santarsiero Donata marcerta di Nicola	figlia	nata 2-10 1906	Arigliano	
6 Santarsiero Carmela fu di Nicola	figlia	nata 22-9	Arigliano	
7 Santarsiero margherita di Nicola	figlia	nata	Arigliano	
8 Santarsiero angela maria di Nicola	figlia	nata 1-10 1910	Arigliano	

IL PREFETTO

Anthony Cardelli

He Can Make a Grown Man Cry: A Memory of Frank Sinatra

He drew tears from grown men's eyes. That's how strong his feelings moved through the audience that night. He told us he just recorded one of the songs from a musical play and wasn't too sure of the lyrics, so he had the sheet music in front of him. The orchestra began the song, and he sang the lyrics from the sheet. It was beautiful to listen to him sing while reading the music and lyrics. The title of the song was "Good Thing Going." It is one of my favorite memories in the darkroom of my mind. A young lady in front of me was so emotional, that there were tears flowing from her eyes, as they were from mine. He can make a grown man cry.

A Theory

I always thought when you take a step back, you would be behind everyone else. But I was deep into my thinking one day and came up with a theory. Taking one step back from the line of life, you would be able to see clearly where everyone else is going. Now, the gap you left when you stepped back will be a breeze to slip through and walk ahead, because you'll know definitely when to turn away from the maddening crowd without being stepped, and you can reach your goal without stepping on anyone's toes.

A Man of Many Dreams

"TT"

One of the best parts of my life was knowing and spending so much time with my best friend "TT" (Thomas Argenti). He said it stood for "Terrible Tom." He missed his calling, because he made people laugh. Not at him; we laughed with him. He always had a punch line. He was a natural. Every funny story had no profanity. He left Trenton in 1949 and went to Atlantic City and got a job at the 500 Club. One time, "Skinny", who was the owner of the club, said to him, "Go up on the stage in the bar room, and tell a story to make us laugh."

I was there, and he started out with, "Hi everybody. Skinny asked me to come up here and say something funny, and if you laugh, he was going to give me a break and then he would give me the clutch," He went on and on, and people laughed when he mentioned all the parts that are needed to build an automobile, adding different stories about how he came to the 500 Club one day and all the years that followed. They were great years, and I'll treasure them as long as I'm inhaling and exhaling. Every now and then when he comes to mind, happy tears fall out and a smiling face.

500 Club, Atlantic City, NJ
At Center: Owner of the 500 Club "Skinny" Paul D'Amato
Far Right: "TT" Thomas Argenti

500 Club, Atlantic City, NJ

Thomas Argenti "TT" Maitre d' of the 500 Club
standing with "Slim" the doorman

Sinatra Performing at the 500 Club, Atlantic City, NJ

Left: Vic Damone with "TT" Thomas Argenti at 500 Club, Atlantic City, NJ

Sinatra having dinner backstage at the 500 Club, Atlantic City, NJ

1960's Sinatra & Dean Martin performing at the 500 Club, Atlantic City, NJ

Dean Martin & Jerry Lewis 500 Club, Atlantic City, NJ

"TT" Thomas Argenti at the 500 Club, Atlantic City, NJ with World Heavy Weight Champion Arnold Raymond Cream better known as "Jersey Joe Walcott"

Entertainers at the 500 Club, Atlantic City, NJ

500 Club, Atlantic City, NJ Left: Willie D'Amato, Phil Brito & "TT" Thomas Argenti

Sammy Davis, Jr. & Johnny Ray at the 500 Club, Atlantic City, NJ

500 Club, Atlantic City, NJ "TT" Thomas Argenti, World Featherweight Champion Guglielmo Papaleo, better known as "Willie Pep" nicknamed "Will-o-the Whisp" & Mike Azzaro of Trenton, NJ

500 Club, Atlantic City, NJ From left: Andrew Iavarone "Squarehead", Dominick Argenti "Crow", Joe DiOrio, Thomas Argenti "TT" & Virgil D'Andrea

A Man of Many Dreams

ANTHONY MARTELLONI
AN AMERICAN HERO

My very good friend, Private First Class Anthony A. Martelloni, 42108576, Company "G", 303d Infantry Regiment, received the "Purple Heart" and "Silver Star" for his gallantry in action at Barnau, Germany, on April 30, 1945. In the vicinity of this town, elements of a rifle platoon were pinned down by a heavy volume of hostile machine gun fire and with no thought of personal safety, he got to his feet and with such fury assaulted the hostile position that two of the enemy were killed, two others captured and the remainder forced to withdraw. This bold action enabled troops of the platoon to kill three more of the enemy as they attempted to disengage themselves. The gallantry displayed on this occasion reflects high credit upon himself and the Armed Forces. Entered military service from New Jersey.

"Heroism feels it never reasons. That's why it's always right."
Tony Martelloni, my friend, An American Hero.

From Left: Tony Martelloni, Myself & Cousin Joey Telesca

THE SUMMER OF 98'

The Summer of 98', what a Summer! I was singing four nights a week. Friday, Saturday, Sunday and Monday. A great place to dine with a beautiful view of the bay and great sunsets. The place was called Marion's. It was located in Margate, New Jersey on the strip. Jerry Blavat, the "geator with the heater", Steve & Cookies, The Dock and old reliable, Maynard's were all there. One Sunday night who walks in none other than Ms. Natalie Cole. It was around 1:00 a.m. and she danced to my singing. She was amazed that I was in the pocket on every Sinatra arrangement. She wrote a note on one of my business cards and planted a big kiss on the card and signed it. This was the first time I ever was complimented from a Pro. One other time, Mr. Sinatra's violinist, Mr. Tony Bosch and his wife were having lunch at Diamond's Restaurant in Trenton. I was setting up for the night's entertainment. The owner mentioned that I sing many Sinatra songs and he asked me if I had the music for the song "It Was a Very Good Year". I pulled it right out of my hat and when I was on the last note, he and his wife stood up and gave me heatie applause. Then he said to me, that my phasing was equal to the "Chairman of the Board."

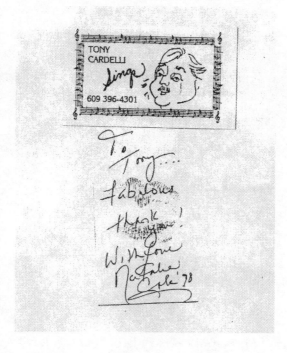

A Man of Many Dreams

To My Friends at Caesars Forum Lounge, Atlantic City, New Jersey 2004

When you reach a certain age, past seventy-five, you explain how you feel by quoting the words of the wise. Someone once said, "You never get a second chance to make a good first impression." I lived my life with that thought and agreed. But for the past two years, and the staff on the special third floor, with a beautiful view of the boardwalk and the beach and the waves rushing to the shore, I take back the agreement of the wise, because you people have given me that second chance. I'll have all the beautiful memories tucked away in my heart, as I move on in another direction. Thank you for the wonderful send-off, which, by the way, completely surprised me!

Truly Your Friend Always,
Tony Cardelli

House Arrest

All of my life, I went through so many dangers. That's par for a true Gemini, most people say that's the way I am. But a Gemini can be anyone he or she desires to be. One minute, I'm as lonely as a book on top of a dusty shelf. The next minute, I'm the life of the party. I can go deep into a shell, put myself in house arrest. Avoid going to football games, thinking every time they get into a huddle, they're talking about me. Many times, I shower, shave, and dress to kill. When I get to open the door and walk to the car, I turn around, go back into the house, change into my PJs, turn on the TV, and watch repeated movies. I fall asleep on the couch, wake up around 12:30 a.m., and go into the bedroom to sleep through another exciting day.

MY ANNA

Anna Migliaccio, Born June 29, 1935

A Man of Many Dreams

MY ANNA

Anna: it was always Anna. Since the first day I noticed and felt her presence. She would always catch me looking at her. Even in a crowded place, she felt my eyes on her, and she would come over to me smiling and ask, "What are you looking at?

And I would always answer, "Beauty." Her eyes were a shade lighter than the night, her hair light brown, and skin smooth and fair.

The year was 1950, during summer vacation. She was going into first-year high. She asked me to cut her hair close all around and shape into a DA in the back. Her hair had a tremendous amount of density, so I cut it in vertical lines. We became good friends, but deep inside, I knew when she became old enough, I wasn't going to let her get away.

A year later, I had to close my barbershop and answer the call from Uncle Sam. I did the last ten months of my two-year hitch in Korea. When I came back, I reopened the barbershop and began adjusting to civilian life. I was twenty-four and single. That is up until the night I was in a local restaurant, having dinner, and felt a tap on my shoulder. I turned around to see who it was, and there she was, beautiful as ever, smiling at me. She asked, "What are you looking at?"

And I answered, "Beauty." We embraced each other, and from that moment on, I never let go. It was so natural being together. We both broke all ties and saw each other every day until death did we part.

We had a beautiful life in the beginning. Catherine Ann added the real meaning of our marriage. We took her everywhere. There wasn't anything she didn't have. All the material things we had plenty, and she was loved to the heavens. Anna dressed her in nothing but designer labels. She cut her hair, and she always was dressed beautifully.

I miss my wife; I miss the life we shared. I miss the sound of her being around. I miss being in love: its warm feeling. I miss the tender loving care she rendered. I miss the "look" when she wanted me. I miss holding her in my arms. I miss falling into a deep sleep. I miss her humor. I miss listening

Anthony Cardelli

to her reason with our daughter. And the grandchildren: how she loved them. Especially when Anthony would walk through the door, she would light up like a Christmas tree. How she adored him. I ask myself a thousand times a day, "Why am I the leftover?" She would have been so proud of Anthony, with his baseball feats and growing into manhood. Elizabeth's personality, her great performance at the G.A.A. show, graduating from high school and entering college. And of course DeAnna, developing into such a beauty. I know Anna is with us. I sense and feel her around the house. Her spirit leaves signs of her presence. I miss my wife; I miss the life we shared, miss walking along the beach after the sun disappeared, miss the vacations at Long Beach Island. I miss the aroma of her cooking on holidays, baking with her friends through the night. I miss my wife. I miss the life we shared; miss the fun we had working together in our hair salon, Heads You Win; miss the dining after work in the restaurants in "the 'Burg." We didn't miss one; our favorite was Greco's. She kept my sanity without her during the early years I would have been lost if she gave up on me. I made so many stupid moves, but she rolled with the punches, met me head-on, and always stopped me in my tracks. I know I'll never have all the things I miss, but her memories I will cherish until I meet her again. Every song I sing is to her memory and the beautiful gift I received from her for over thirty-seven years of our marriage and the young years of her life as a teenager, when I first met her. She was fifteen when I cut her hair in a D.A. style. I was twenty, but I didn't date her until I was twenty-four, and she was nineteen going on twenty. I pray she is here in spirit and leaves little signs of her being. I sense her being in our house. I feel she is still there. I miss my wife; I miss the life we shared.

A Man of Many Dreams

MY GRANDSON ANTHONY HIS DAY IN THE SUN

I had the time of my life from the moment he was born. When I think of the early years, happy tears drop out of my eyes. All the photographs that were taken, I kept the negatives in the darkroom of my mind. They keep developing in front of my eyes, like the scenes from T-ball through American Legion. I regret working the day he hit two home runs in one inning and two more to follow. The box score roared. It was played out of town, in the middle of the week. He called me after the game. I was in my barbershop, and he said, "Pop Pop, I hit four home runs and a single." He made two home runs in one inning. His first home run with the bases empty, the second home run with one runner on. His third home run with two runners on and his fourth home run with the bases loaded which made it a Grand Slam. His fifth time at bat he hit a single. His total batted in was five for five with ten runs batted in. That year in 1994, he made the National High School Record Book for Baseball. He wore the number nine and what do you know—if you look up the book, he's next to the one and only Ted Williams. Williams hit two home runs in one inning. Anthony's record is recorded as four home runs, the cycle, and ten runs batted in.

Although I had always wished I was there that day, I realize now I was there all along. My grandson, "His Day in the Sun."

A Man of Many Dreams

TIME WITHOUT A LENGTH

Time, without a length, flies. In a split second, I can go back to the corner, flipping a coin and coming up with Heads You Win, the new and last name of my hair salon. It was my last shot of staying in business, where my wife and I settled the past. We didn't break even. I did more crazy things, but we agreed to get down to business and leave the past where it belongs: behind us.

The year was 1979. We had a two-year-old grandson and a one-year-old granddaughter. We devoted ourselves to them; top priority in our lives. Nothing else was more important than to see they had a future. Anthony and Elizabeth; and before you knew it, DeAnna came along in 1980. Anthony and Elizabeth were thirteen months apart, and DeAnna was three years younger than the firstborn. I was having the time of my life, never refusing to take care of them when asked. They stayed over so many times, it got so they would come in and beg for a bath so they could sleep over. I would take them to school, ball games, movies, and doctor's appointments . . .

ONLY TIME WILL TELL

I've tasted the bitter and sweet of life. The best and the worst of times. God-made things weren't enough for man and woman. We wanted more than the moon, the sun, the clouds, the trees, the rivers, the lakes, the oceans. God provided the means to survive. It was all here on earth for us to find. We still haven't learned that the only thing He wanted in return was peace on earth for all mankind. He gave us a world so vast, with so much room and then some to share. True, He didn't make it easy for us. He put us through the test, and we failed. It is now 2006, where we are going from here we know all to well, only time will tell.

Anthony Cardelli

Dear Anthony and Jillian

I was sitting in my living room and looking at the photographs you gave me of Gianna Marie, beautiful Gianna Marie. Every time I think of her, a warm feeling rushes through me, and a great, big smile draws happy tears. You two have brought me the happiness that will make up the rest of my life, what it lacked in the length of it. To make a long story short, I had my share of loneliness since July 15, 1991, but your mother kept my sanity, along with Elizabeth, DeAnna, and you, Anthony, and the wonderful gift we all received on July 23, 2007.

The Fourth Generation
Beginning of "Our Family Tree"

Anthony, Jillian & Gianna Marie Ciccia

Living My Dream
Elizabeth's Wedding Day, June 27, 2009

Jeppy & Elizabeth

Myself, Anthony, Gianna & Jeppy

Anthony Cardelli

LIVING MY DREAM

I think back when I was twenty, I looked at sixty years ahead of me. I'm closer to the year eighty now, and I'm looking at only tomorrow in front of me. But all the tomorrows will make up in my life for the lack of its length. A few pages back, I wrote about when I was a client of Dr. Marin, who advised me to stop smoking if I wanted to see my first granddaughter walk down the aisle with her dad. I quit when I was forty-eight, but not completely. It was with his advice that I finally kicked the habit. What a wonderful gift to be living your dream. Now, seeing my great-granddaughter is helping me to continue "My Dream."

MUSIC TO MY EARS

I've been called many names through the years by friends, foes, and peers. Only one made these old, hazel eyes pour with happy tears. And that was when Anthony, Elizabeth, and DeAnna called me "Pop-Pop." Now, who in the world could top that? None other than Miss Gianna Marie, if I'm still here, to call me Great-Grand Pop!

SOMEONE ONCE SAID

Someone once said: Happiness makes up in life what it lacks in length. I had my share of happiness throughout my life and it's true it was short lived, but someone came into this world and dried up all the sad tears I shedded throughout the years in the past. And the length of the happiness I feel will last as long as I'm on this earth. Ms. Gianna Marie has given me back the future to look forward to. Living the present and leaving the past where it belongs, behind me. I'm looking forward of not renewing my lease and moving back closer to my family. I want to get to know my grandchildren, my daughter and Jeppy and of course my great-granddaughter and future great-grandchildren as long as I'm able.

My Love to Sing

1950's performing at the Columbus Lounge, Trenton, NJ with Anna behind me and Mr. Gordon at piano

Anthony Cardelli

MY LOVE TO SING

I was ten years old in 1939 when I first heard Sinatra sing and that was it. I remember that first record like it was yesterday. He was with the Harry James Orchestra and the guys had cut "All or Nothing at All" and "From the Bottom of My Heart." I knew the second that double-sided hit came on that this was the music for me. I started attending Sinatra concerts in 1944. I would play hooky from school and get a ride to Philadelphia or New York from my Trenton home and I would follow the bobby-soxers who were our dream girls. I would happily sit in the Paramount Theater in New York from 6 o'clock at night just to watch each stage show Sinatra headlined. I've attended Frank's concerts dozens of times over the decades. I've never taken a music lesson. Not for my singing, not for playing, and not for appreciation. I cannot even read music. I studied him carefully, learning his phrasing and memorizing his records. I give him all the credit.

After Frank came Tony Bennett and Dean Martin and Billie Holiday. I didn't have any illusions of being a big star. I had fun entertaining where ever I performed. I'm just a local singer and people seem to like it. I always enjoyed singing . . . it takes me out of a lot of things . . . It's for myself. I'm selfish I guess.

I began singing since the age of 17 but it wasn't until 1959 that I began singing professionally with several jazz and pop groups, most notably with quartets led by Ernie Butcher and Tony Spair. My first gig was at the Columbus Lounge in downtown Trenton with the Ernie Butcher Trio. There was Ernie Butcher on tenor, Butch Brenfleck at the drums and Joe Knapp on the organ and piano. I sang with trios until the late seventies. Then, in 1989, I decided to design an act featuring tunes associated with Sinatra. I sang to a recorded background of tasty big band arrangements, many orchestrated by Al Raymond. This allowed me to pick up my singing career and gave me the opportunity to perform once again. From there I performed in numerous restaurants from my neighborhood and throughout all of New Jersey and Pennsylvania.

For me Sinatra expresses the triumphs and tragedies of human emotions. I know I'll never be as talented as Frank Sinatra, but what I want to do is help keep his music alive for future generations. To me, that's as much as anybody could possibly want to achieve.

1970's Entertaining at Weinberg's Clothing Store, South Broad Street, Trenton, NJ: On Bass is Frank Herrera & Dick Braytenbah on Piano

MY MUSIC

A Man of Many Dreams

MY MUSIC

When ever I'm feeling low,
I pick myself up with a song
For me and My Music,
Keep me rolling along
With the clouds drifting by
Catching a star to chart my way

A SONG I'D LIKE TO SING

My song is a song I'd like to sing
Because I wrote the lyrics and set them to music
Words with sound for all seasons
Yes, my song is the song I like to sing
I laid down the beat on the very first note
And picked up the temple as I went along
Added rhythm to the lyrics of my song

IT SURE FEELS GOOD

It sure feels good when it comes out right
No matter how many times you try
When you finally get it right,
It makes all the other times so worthwhile
It sure feels good after paying your dues,
With a million one-nighters
Taking your bows when the curtain calls
Taking the boos when the curtain falls

Anthony Cardelli

UNDER THE BIG TOP

Under the big top
Painted faces of circus clowns
Creates a musical score with the sound of children's laughter
And lyrics from the lion's roar
Keeping in tempo to the crack of the trainer's whip

A crescendo of strings
Zing through the net below the high wire
As the flying trapeze soar under the big top

Painted faces of the circus clowns
Smeared with tears from the sawdust in their eyes
With each tear that drops will never rust on the love and trust
Through the eyes of the painted faces of the circus clowns

SAME OLD SONG

I sang the same old song once too often
If I don't change my tune, they'll be leaving me soon
Then I'll be left with nobody to sing to
Because nobody wants to listen to a song they already heard
I'll start with fresh lyrics
Words with reason
With a voice well seasoned
Resounding from the Heavens
Bouncing off the peaks above the clouds
Soaring through into thin air
Gliding down to a sail
Leaving a trail for all to follow

A Man of Many Dreams

I'M NOT READY

I'm not ready for Freddy
So tell Sam to keep pouring on the ham
'Cause I'm not ready to sing My Swan Song
I still want to keep paying my dues
I'm not ready to snap my string of one-nighters
As long as the applause drowns out the boos,
There's still more to gain then to lose

A TRIBUTE TO SINATRA AND HIS MUSIC

Hoboken Four

A Man of Many Dreams

ALTHOUGH WE NEVER MET

Although we never met, I always felt that we did
Because from the moment I first heard musical notes from his lips,
I knew it was the beginning of a beautiful musical friendship

The year was 1939
The sound of Hitler's storm troopers were goose-stepping across the River
Rhine
I was ten years young, listening to "The Kid from Hoboken,"
Who crossed the River Hudson on a four-cent ferry ride

With just a few tokens to spare, he transferred onto a bus,
Standing up front with a mic in his hand
And stretched its cord from Englewood to Hollywood
Giving his "All or Nothing at All" from the bottom of his heart,
With the James Boys Band
And that's how the whole damn beautiful musical friendship began!

A Man of Many Dreams

The Paramount

The Paramount
Rocked with Bobby Soxers jumping up and down
Anxiously waiting for the show to start

Ushers were standing by with an amble supply of smelling salts
Ready to apply to all those who wouldn't survive,
The sight of his baby blue eyes

The year was 1944
We were too young to go to war
Too old to play kick the can

The Paramount
Rocked with Bobby Soxers jumping up and down
Hysterically waiting for the show to start
I was there wearing a pair wrapped around My Heart

(Written 1982)

A Man of Many Dreams

BOBBY SOCKS

Bobby Socks you don't have to wear
These Old Blue Eyes can see you are still out there
Although time has changed the color of your hair
And added a touch of makeup here and there,
You should see how beautiful you are from up here
Through the glare of the spotlights,
These Old Blue Eyes see the beauty time can never take away

Dressed in an evening gown
With a silver crown framing your face
He feels the warmth from your embrace of the past four decades
These Old Blue Eyes never will they fade

Bobby Socks you don't have to wear
You don't have to jump up and down
To let me know you're still around
I can still hear the sound in my ear
When the Paramount rocked around the block
Reminding me of those wonderful years

So just in case you lost or misplaced them,
Don't ever stop coming to see me every night
Because right from the start, up until now,
I carry the original pair in My Heart!

A Man of Many Dreams

THE PIED PIPER'S SERENADE

They followed him everywhere
Inhaling the music he filtered through the air
Exhaling from their hearts the sound of his voice,
For all the world to share
With a voice well seasoned, reciting words with reason
He phases the lyrics keeping everyone in step from the tempo he sets

He sowed the seeds from composers of the past
And reharvested their melodies into "Golden Classics"
No one but him could parlay a four-cent ferry ride across the Hudson,
Hop on a bus with the James Boys Band,
Standing up front with a mic in his hand,
Cross a span from Englewood to Hollywood,
And stretch a string of one-nighters wider than the Missouri
To fame and all its glory!

Paying his dues gracefully
And bowing to the applause, along with the boos
"Francis Albert Sinatra"
"The Kid from Hoboken"
Didn't sit on his hands and hope to be crowned,
"The Singing Pope"!

A Man of Many Dreams

A ROCK-A-DOLLY

A rock-a-dolly
In the middle of a chorus line with the Ziegfeld Follies
Keeping in step with the future Rockettes
Never missing her mark on stage
Far from view of the spotlight's glare

Although time has changed the color of her hair
And added a few wrinkles here and there
A rock-a-dolly from the Ziegfeld Follies is still kicking her heels
And keeping in step with the younger set,
On a Broadway stage with the New York Rockettes
Second from the left, out of sight from the spotlight's glare
She beams a smile that melts your heart
Through the heavy makeup she wears

Sinatra's Wedding Day to Nancy Barbato, February 4, 1939

Anthony Cardelli

Since One Million BC

Since one million BC, up until now
It's a miracle when I think,
Of all that time the world was spinning around and around
Just to finally stop for you and me
Time tried so hard to be unkind to you
But its efforts were in vain
You look exactly the same
All the beauty you have inside, time couldn't pass by
It came to a full stop

Anthony Cardelli

BIG RED APPLE

The legend lives under the "Big Apple" in the sky
Baking in the sun all through the day
Then when twilight comes it cools down to an amber glow,
To set the stage

There's a Big Red Apple in the sky
Baking in the sun, running its juices
Burning with energy that runs all over the city

The legend lives, it comes alive,
When the sun turns to twilight
And the moon brightens up the night,
Along the Great White Way!

Anthony Cardelli

OLD BLUE EYES

Ring a ding ding
The New Year in
With "Old Blue Eyes"
Belting and banging the old year out
With "I've Got You Under My Skin"
And a flight through the night on "Trilogy Road"
A distance from then, now and when

Old Blue Eyes keep shining through
Keep shining through the darkness
To light the way of Hearts
Young and gay, old and gray

SONGS TO SING

Did you ever stop to think what the world would be like
If there were no songs to sing?
Birds would just fly around all day and do nothing
People would talk in the shower
And everyone would just sit around for hours,
Listening to Eddie Fisher records
But thank Heaven there are songs to sing!

A Man of Many Dreams

SILENT BEAUTY

It's all over but the shouting
But as I sit in silence with the roar of the crowd ringing in my ears
With each teardrop smearing the greasepaint streaming down my face,
Washing away the years of hiding behind a disguise of false impressions

It's all over but the shouting
I can still hear the roar of the crowd ringing in my ear
It's all over but the vibrations I feel from the standing ovations
From the sound of the applause beating in my heart
It's all over but the silence
Seeing in slow motion, teardrops from the eyes of a circus clown

MY SWAN SONG

It's much too early for My Swan Song
I've got so many more to sing
I still feel I haven't covered everything
And I doubt I ever will
So, I'll continue as long as I can
In my own way
Up front with a mic in my hand

Leading an all-star band
With the rhythm of Riddle
The swinging of Basie
Ray Brown thumbing on bass
George Benson on guitar
And the strings of Costa
Now that's as tasty as mama's pasta
On a Sunday afternoon

A Man of Many Dreams

OLD BLUE EYES IS BACK

"Old Blue Eyes" is back
Back where he belongs
Standing up front with a mic in his hand
Singing the same old songs
He stepped back from the stage and glaring lights
And called time-out to see what was going on inside
And within a short while after looking around,
In his search, this is what he found

In the past four decades Old Blue Eyes felt
All the beauty his shallow eyes had missed
And from the beauty he's bringing joy forever,
With his singing message
To the old to stay young and the young to keep their youth

Old Blue Eyes is back
Back where he belongs
Standing up front with a mic in hand
And a crescendo of strings
Swinging with the Basie Band
Back doing what he does so well
Dwelling in a whirlpool of melodies
With each song he picks from his bouquet of classics
He can do no wrong

Yes, Old Blue Eyes is back where he belongs
The critics who claimed he was just a fad.
Are long gone in the past
For Old Blue Eyes will never fade or fail to feel,
The love spent in the past four decades year after year!

Anthony Cardelli

THE CHAIRMAN OF THE BOARD

He sings the same old songs
But with reason now
He sings the same old songs
But with a voice well seasoned now

He rearranged his bouquet of standards
And transcended them into classics
With the seeds planted from composers of the past
He outlasted the critics who swarmed over the fields he sowed
And left them starving for the Golden Harvest he reaped

William B. Williams named him
"The Chairman of the Board"
Truer words were never spoken!

THE KID FROM HOBOKEN

He sings the same old songs with reason now, with a voice well seasoned now. Mixed in a whirlpool of melodies with sad and happy tears he gathered through the years. A bouquet of pearls, emeralds, and wheat for the whole world to feast on the flavors of love songs sung, with a never-ending appetite to grow young.

The memories he carries with him on his immense journey through life keep developing from the negatives stored deep in the darkroom of his mind. It shows all over him the moment he steps on stage. Positive prints of the past forty years flash through the audience, on a laser beam vibrating "From the Bottom of His Heart." Giving his "All or Nothing at All" ever since the day he parlayed a four-cent ferry ride across the Hudson and hopped on a bus with the James Boys Band, standing up front with a mic in his hand, and stretched its cord from Englewood to Hollywood, paying his dues in between with a string of one-nighters. "The Kid from Hoboken" didn't sit on his hands and hope for three puffs of white smoke. He worked twenty-four hours a day to become the "Singing Pope."

Sinatra performing at the 500 Club, Atlantic City, NJ with Joey Bishop behind the curtain & Bill Miller at Piano

Anthony Cardelli

TO A MAN I NEVER MET

He's been through good times, bad times, happy times, and sad times
He's been applauded, he's been booed, shot down, and wooed
He sat with kings but never lost the common touch
And when things were rough, he went back on the bus,
With the boys in the band to cross a span of one-nighters

And when the smoke turned black, he didn't wait for it to clear,
By sitting on his hands and hope for

He is a professional in every way
And that is why music lovers of today call him the "Singing Pope"

"God blessed your lifetime, Francis Albert Sinatra"!

MY DREAMS

Anthony Cardelli

My Dreams

My dreams are overdue
And yet, I believe before I leave,
They will all come true
I still have the will to find the way
For I believe Rome wasn't built in a day

Time has half past me by
Two score and ten have come to an end
From the beginning of my first outcry
With the slap of the midwife's hand

My dreams are overdue
Lady luck keeps passing me by
But I believe one day luck will see me through all my dreams
And all my dreams will come true

A Man of Many Dreams

A Fisherman's Dream

Rainbows rising over horizons
Glittering waves of silver and gold
Arched across the skies
Running downstream
To spawn in the brook
Before caught on the hook
Of a Fisherman's Dream

The Legend Lives On

The legend lives on
It comes alive when the Big Apple in the sky shines at it best

All My Dreams are way overdue
But I keep dreaming they'll all come true
I search each day with a new pair of eyes with 20-20 vision
Up in the sky and among the many stars,
Shining beyond my time and place
I feel one will fall out from space,
To chart the way for me to follow

Anthony Cardelli

DREAMERS

In 1945, I was betwixt
With my dreams tapped at both ends
Pouring out fantasies up the river
And reality running down streams into a well
Wishing all my dreams come true
What do dreamers do when they don't dream anymore?
What makes them carry on?
What makes them break the silence with a song?

I was a dreamer
I used to dream every night
And wake up dreaming through the day until twilight
The time I used to spend searching with a new pair of eyes,
As the sun was setting in the west

What do dreamers do when they stop dreaming?
Do they settle for second best?
And step aside to let the leaders go by?
Do dreamers who don't dream anymore,
Stop searching when they close their eyes?
What do dreamers do?
Do they settle for not dreaming anymore?

A Man of Many Dreams

I DON'T DREAM LIKE THAT ANYMORE

It didn't matter what time it was
Morning, noon, or night
My dream was always there, always in view
Never left my sight, never late, never early
Always on time, constantly on my mind
I carried it with me, wherever I went
Never too heavy, never too light

All over me it showed
Through the darkness of the night
A beautiful glow but that was along time ago
Since you closed the door,
I don't dream like that anymore

I USED TO DREAM

I used to dream about a house on a hill
Surrounded with trees
Rich with fruit to pick at will
Grassy hillocks to lay and rest
Shaded from the sun in a cool Love Nest
This dream was an illusion of grandeur
I don't dream like that anymore

I used to dream this house was full
Not an inch of space was there room for hate
Flavors of Love was ours to taste
A daily recipe we mixed and ready to pour
I don't dream like that anymore

Anthony Cardelli

NIGHT NURSE

Night nurse watch over me
Don't leave me alone too long
Check in once in a while
I need your smile to help me forget the pain

Night nurse watch over me
Don't leave me alone too long
Check in once in a while
I need your tender loving care
To bare the pain through the long lonely night

I need the sound of your laughter
And the smile that goes with it
Night nurse dressed in white

A Man of Many Dreams

ARE YOU JUST A DREAM?

Are you just a dream that never really comes true?
Are you here to stay or just passing through?
Because I've been searching ever since I saw a vision
Beyond my time and place
A vision I can feel now
From my hands touching your face!

NOW IS THE TIME

Now is the time
To make all of Our Dreams come true
Now is the time
To stop what we're doing
And search with our eyes
And listen to those resounding voices from Paradise

THE SONG FROM OUR DREAM

The beat of your heart is in time with mine
We're both skipping a line here and there
We both skip a note here and there
Then after we filled in all the notes that we skipped
And completed the lyrics,
We're ready to sing the song from our dream

We'll build a house on a hill and surround it with flowers galore
Whatever the four seasons blow the willows will bend, the oak will stand tall
The leaves will fall in autumn to bed down the roots before winter's snow
The evergreens will withstand the freezing rains

Anthony Cardelli

LET ME INTO YOUR DREAM

Let me into your dream
Let me make it come true
I've been searching for such a long time
For someone whose dream is the same as mine

Let me build our house high on a hill
Surround it with trees rich with fruit and leaves
Fill it with love in every room to call our very own
With a special recipe that makes a home

Let me into your dream
Let me make it come true
This I swear to you I can easily do
'Cause I'm a one-time loser, too
Together we can refill that empty house with whatever love we have left
Which will be more than enough because it's yours and mine alone
The perfect recipe to make it our home

The next time the world turns on a bright sunny day
I'm gonna do my best to keep it that way
If given the chance to start our hearts to beat as one,
The sun would rise to the sound of birds on the wing
Dropping each note through powder-puff clouds
On beautiful rainbow towels waving in the wind
If given the chance to start our hearts to beat as one,
The moon would silently appear out of the tranquility of twilight
And spread a bouquet of red and yellow roses over the stars

A Man of Many Dreams

Let me into your dream
Together we will make them come true in time
For the dreams I see through your eyes are the same as mine
A house on a hill surrounded with willows and oak
To bend and stand tall against the knee level winds of life
A garden with planted flowers galore
A welcome wreath hanging on the front door
Watching our vineyards grow along with our offsprings,
Who will show all the love within
And as we grow old together as our hair colors gray,
We will feel in our hearts as we felt on our wedding day
So young and gay

Anthony Cardelli

MY FAVORITE DREAM

I always save my favorite dream for last
Because it's all about you
It begins on the first day we met
And continues the whole night through
Up until the moment I open my eyes
And feel you by my side

My favorite dream always comes true
It's not like the rest that are way overdue
Lost somewhere in the past
That's why I always save my favorite dream for last

For every scene is real
Nothing is staged
Everything on every page are parts unrehearsed
We wrote the book with each other's hearts!

1958-1960 with Anna & her sister Agnes Migliaccio
at the Columbus Lounge, Trenton, NJ

MY NEIGHBORHOOD

1945 at DeLorenzo's Tomato Pie, Hudson Street, Trenton, NJ with friends

1946 at Dominick Pica's Tomato Pie, Whittaker Avenue, Trenton, NJ with Agabiti Club Members: Left: Myself, Danny Marazzo "The Brains", Benny Burzachiello & Standing Left: Cousin Nick Valli & Far Right: Mike Azzaro

A Man of Many Dreams

MY NEIGHBORHOOD

What they call a ghetto today,
Was once my neighborhood
A place where one common language was clearly understood
Every door on the block was kept unlocked
Friends and strangers alike never bothered to knock
For all hearts were open to share their tables
Breaking bread, drinking homemade wine
In a time when, what was mine, was yours
What is now, is an illusion of grandeur

WHERE I WAS BORN

The place where I was born is still the same
Nothing's changed, as strange as it may seem in this day and age
Since my first out cry after the slap from the midwife's hand
The rest of the world turned upside down
And crashed with a roar out of the Twenties
Except the place where I was born

The people there took it in strive
And rolled with the punches to soften the blows
They bended to knee level winds
But stood their ground, excepting charity
Carrying in their soul the Original Sin
Believing Our Lord, Jesus Christ would reappear on earth,
To heal all the suffering in the world

1930's with my cousins, Felix (Phillip), Myself & Nicolas Telesca

1940's with grandmom, my aunts & my Santarsiero cousins, Lucille Panettieri, Felix Melleno, Diane Filidore, Matilda Valli, Rosemarie Valli, Phyllis Nicolai, Douglas Filidore, Catherine Telesca, Santina Nicolai & Josephine Valli

1950 Left: Phyllis DeVito D'Andrea, my Anna Migliaccio
& Lorraine Rossi

1945 Cousin Joey Telesca & Myself

1945-1950 On Swan Street, Trenton, NJ with
Tony Martelloni driving, Myself & friends

1945-1950 At Seaside Heights, NJ Left: Myself, Dominick Argenti "Crow",
Thomas Argenti "TT" & Andrew Iavarone "Squarehead"

A Man of Many Dreams

TWO SILHOUETTES

Two silhouettes dancing on a disc
High over the rooftops of the Stacy Trent and Hotel Hildebrecht
People came from near and afar
To watch in amazement as they waltz under the stars
I don't remember the year but the night was bright
With the moon beaming and a smile on their faces

Two silhouettes dancing on a disc
High over the rooftops of the Stacy Trent and Hotel Hildebrecht
Under the spotlight of a full flower moon
Spreading a bouquet of yellow roses
Along the banks of the Delaware
One Summer night in June

As they danced under the spotlight's glare,
Following every move they dare
Each step they danced under a galaxy of stars
Brought them closer to Jupiter and Mars
Two silhouettes dancing on a disc
High over the rooftops of the Stacy Trent and Hotel Hildebrecht

TRENTON 1939

Dancing on a disc mounted on a flag pole defining death with every step
Blowing a kiss in the wind
Two silhouettes in a spin under the gazing stars
Fox-trotting their way to Mars
Under the spotlight's glare following every move they dare
Casting shadows from the glow of the moon into the crowd below

Anthony Cardelli

THE MIDWIFE

She lived in a tenement full of life in every room
On every floor of unlocked doors
For the midwife, all hearts were open to her
She was working around the clock
She was made from good stock
To save time she didn't bother to knock
She was heavyset, but dead set walking up a flight of stairs
Carrying her wares to a mother with child
Boiling hot water on the stove
She spoke one language everyone understood
In a time and place that is now called a ghetto
Was then a neighborhood

With the slap of her hand
The outcry of the newborn brought up happy tears from within
Drowning out the sorrows in the sound of the trail of sad tears
Running over in the past

Mother with child labors through the night
With the helping hands of the midwife
To deliver the divine gift of life!

A Man of Many Dreams

MY SONG

"My Song"
When are they going to start singing "My Song"
I wrote it way back then in time
When people broke into tears
When they had to break a nickel
A time of depression

A time when a doctor was called a midwife
A time when one language was clearly understood
A time when a ghetto was called a neighborhood
A time when every door on the block was unlocked

There was always room for one more to break bread with
Pouring the wine and sharing God's Table
Somewhere beyond my time,
Such a place in time will come around again

THE TWENTIES

The Twenties
Came roaring in like a lion
Knocking over everything
Like a bull running loose in a store full of chinaware
A decade of mixed emotions and illusions
Along with the sounds of Porter and Van Heusen
Adding to the confusion of an overcrowded society

CABARET SHOW AT THE KENT ATHLETIC ASSOCIATION CLUB 1960'S

Left: Fred DeVito, Jr., Myself & Tony Merlino

Left: Andrew DeVito, Sr., Tony Merlino, Fred DeVito, Jr. & Myself

Performing at the Kent AA Cabaret Show 1960's

Far left is myself with Kent AA members performing at the Cabaret Show 1960's

Far right is myself with Kent AA members performing at the Cabaret Show 1960's

From left: Myself, Frank Cimini, Joe Tuccillo & last Joe Chiarrello

A Man of Many Dreams

CHARACTERS FROM MY NEIGHBORHOOD

This story took place in a back room inside a local luncheonette in my neighborhood around 1965, 1970 give or take. I wrote this in 2001.

Pay as you go and you'll never owe. "Why should I pay him? He ain't with nobody. How about the time they beat him for twenty gees on the Dodgers against Baltimore in the Series". The Chicken Man took the bet, twenty big ones. He came to the club to collect the bet from Cut-Eye Louie. The reason they call him Cut-Eye is another story. I will explain later. Everybody is playing cards, there's a knock rummy at one table, five card stud, hearts, one fifty one, and seven card poker at the big round table, seats seven. The Chicken Man spots Cut-Eye Louie at the round table and waits for him to call him over. Ten minutes go by, nothing happens, so the Chicken Man walks over to Cut-Eye and strikes up a conversation with Cut-Eye and gradually mentions the bet. Cut-Eye stops what he's doing and in a loud voice, asks "what the f— are you talking about, what bet? I never called in a bet to you and if I did" . . . he pauses and looks at Blue Eyes sitting across the table:

Cut-Eye: "Blue Eyes, who did I tell you, I liked in the Series?"
Blue Eyes: "Baltimore"
Cut-Eye: "Byrd?"
Bryd: "Baltimore"
Cut-Eye: "J.C?"
J.C.: "Baltimore"
Cut-Eye: "Sticks"
Sticks: "Baltimore"
Cut-Eye: "Ringo?"
Ringo: "Baltimore"
Cut-Eye: "Fry?"
Fry: "Baltimore"

Then, everybody in the room shouts, "Baltimore"!!!

Chicken Man: "Cut-Eye, there's gonna be trouble".
Cut-Eye: "trouble for who?"

Anthony Cardelli

Chicken Man: "Not you, Cut-Eye, trouble for me. I got to go back uptown and take the heat".

Chicken Man goes in the next room, guys who are not connected, wanna-bees, everybody knew who they were. Dressed in tailored made suits, five inch white on white, one hundred percent cotton shirts. Italian hand made shoes, hand painted silk ties. The cycle, horses, cards, craps and what not.

There was another character we called, "Count everybody down Tony". If you don't gamble count everybody down. Tony starting fights in the local bars pushing people around, living high, betting nie, has you pegged for six figures. He knows, may I say, he thinks he knows how much money everybody in his social circle is worth. Everybody knows he has a vivid imagination and that it is a cover up, to throw you off the track on what he is really worth. Like he still has the first dollar he ever earned in one of his shoes.

Another character we called, "Gonna be a big man some day Billy". No matter what day or what occasion, he dresses to kill and tips his hat to all the females. He never has an unkind word to say to anyone. He speaks highly of everyone. When he wins he is very generous and he loses like a gentleman.

Now, there is "Sorry Tom", like Will Rogers, he too never met a man he didn't like. He constantly is sorry for everything in creation.

Then of course there was Cut-Eye Louie, I said earlier that I would explain how he got his nick name. He always bragged he would cut a guy's eye down the middle if he caught a guy flirting with his chick. One night at a social dance, he winks at some chick and her man caught the action. He bolted over with his pocket knife and slit Cut-Eye Louie's eye dead center.

Every neighborhood has a personal barbershop, grocery store, tailor shop, etc. If you want the latest news the local barbershop is the spot. Who's running numbers, who's taking horse bets, sport bets, who's hustling in card games at the social clubs and who's making bets on pool sharks. And the funny part about all of this action is that they all bet among themselves.

A Man of Many Dreams

One day Louie the Lug wins. The next day he gives it all back to Cut-Eye Louie, it could be within the same day. The winner takes everyone to one of the many local restaurants and everybody feasts on the big winner. After they had their fill, it's back to the social club to lay the skit down, meaning craps, and buck against each other throughout the night.

That's the way it was in my neighborhood. My part of town was connected to New York and the north end was connected to Philly. South and west it was give and take. The main guys would try to keep the peace, but the wanna-bees were always the problem.

When I hit the "Big Five O" they had a surprise birthday party at one of the eateries in Chambersburg, Greco's Restaurant. Bertani Amarone 1965 was on the table in front of my plate and everyone shouted for me to make a toast. I got up with my glass of Amarone, thanked everyone and made my speech that went like this: "It's half past my lifetime with more or less than fifty to go, what you see before you is all I have to show. The past is gone, the present is going fast and as far as the future is concerned, now that I have reached the point of no return, I know all to well what amount of energy I have left to burn. Only time will tell."

Yeah, only time will tell. Well, here it is twenty two years later and I am still making the night scene singing in and out of town clubs throughout the state. Making new friends, meeting nice people all over the state.

Anthony Cardelli

Diamond Jim

There are some things money can't buy
But that didn't stop Diamond Jim to give it a try
His philosophy was everyone has a price
So he showered his girls with diamonds and pearls,
To melt their hearts of ice

He rolled up quite a score of maidens and whores,
Throughout his life of being the Hawk
For in the end Jim was left with all his diamonds and all his pearls
And with an empty nest that once was filled with doves,
Ascending to a space without love
There are some things money can't buy

"A Warning to the Friday Night Out Boys": The Battle of Who's Wearing the Pants

He claims he loves me
Yet he wants to be young and free
And keep me under lock and key
He expects me to sit home
While he makes the rounds painting the town
And doesn't want to hear a sound or even a peep out of me

I've taken his jiving long enough
And before it drives me up a wall with the rest of the jitterbugs
I'm changing my name back to the former Ms. Gibbs
And join the ranks of Woman's Lib

A Man of Many Dreams

RICHARD GIZZI

Richard Gizzi, the "Kid from Jersey City"
Is always busy with undivided concentration
Never hesitates one split second on any decision he makes
From behind the chair of tonsorial artistry,
He demonstrates what his colleagues fabricate
With photographs he develops from the negatives in his mind
To positive prints of self-creations,
That are far beyond the imagination of his peers

Richard Gizzi is not one to sit on his hands and hope
He concentrates professionally twenty-four hours a day
He divided amateur into professional and came up with white smoke
Richard Gizzi is a "professional pope"
He became The Chairman of the Board of tonsorial artistry

Anthony Cardelli

TRENTON MAKES, THE WORLD TAKES

"Trenton Makes, the World Takes"
Would light up across the Delaware every night
The Capital City of the Garden State
She's been in business since 1679
One hundred years ahead of her time
Now with three hundred years bound in her history books,
She's declining in her looks

The Father of our Country one Christmas Eve
Made plans to cross the Delaware with all his might
He put up a hell of fight just to sleep over one night
After the first encounter he was taken aback
But went in for the second round
And the battle was won and the turning point made way,
To the freedom all Americans cherish today

February 22, 1989 at the Eagles Tavern, Broad Street,
Trenton, NJ with George & Mayor Holland of Trenton

A Man of Many Dreams

LATITUDE SAILING OFF THE JERSEY SHORE

Latitude sailing off the Jersey Shore
I came upon sights never seen before
With only the stars to chart my way
In search of the treasures,
Buried under the sands of Ole Cape May
And as widows watched from the Top of the Marc
With eyes big as moonbeams dancing on the waves
The clouds cast a shallow over Barnegat Bay

Cape May diamonds sparkling in the sand
Precious stones washed ashore from foreign lands
As widows watch from the Top of the Marc
Their eyes light up from the moon beaming over Barnegat Bay
As the stars set a glow, to chart the way for the sign of a ship
Latitude sailing off the Jersey Shore

You can cast off on a moonbeam shinning over Barnegat Bay
Catch the midnight tide with only the stars to chart your way
Cutting through the clouds, casting shadows on the waves
Latitude sailing to the Top of the Marc down to Ole Cape May

The sun simmered down to a twilight glow
A full flowered moon showed off a bouquet of yellow roses,
Dancing over the waves
Each beam kept in step with only the stars to chart the way
To what was once the Pirate's Paradise

Anthony Cardelli

Down in Ole Cape May
Diamonds sparkle in the sand, a Pirate's Paradise
An oasis for the ships from across the seas that galloped over the waves
With only the stars to chart their way

Late Summer sunrise lifting the wings of seagulls over the tide
High and mighty across the sky they soar every which way
They follow its rays slipping through the clouds
Paring over the waves down in Ole Cape May

Latitude sailing with only the stars to chart my way
Feeling the warmth of the sun on a ship of the sea
Galloping over the waves through the darkness into a bright new day!

A Man of Many Dreams

DIAMONDS IN THE SAND

Casting off on a moonbeam
Shining over Sandy Hook
Catching the outgoing tide
With only the stars to chart my way

Drifting through the clouds
Casting shadows over the waves
A chorus of dancing porpoises in phosphorescent waters
Guided me through the darkness of the night

At break of dawn I caught a glimpse of the light
Reflected from the sun off Barnegat Bay
Latitude sailing down to Ole Cape May
In search of diamonds in the sand

Anthony Cardelli

FROM THE HIGHLANDS DOWN TO OLE CAPE MAY

From the Highlands down to Ole Cape May
New Jersey's got it all the way
Just follow the sun on its one hundred and twenty-six mile run
Shining in a haven of beaches galore
Along the Jersey shore
You can cast off on a moonbeam
And catch the midnight tide rising the ocean's floor
And go latitude sailing with only the stars to chart your way
From the Highlands down to Ole Cape May

Latitude sailing from the Highlands to Ole Cape May
Casting off on a moonbeam shining over Barnegat Bay
Latitude sailing with only the stars to chart my way
Sailing over the waves until the break of dawn
To follow the sun as it rises over a haven of beaches galore
Off the Jersey Shore!

A Man of Many Dreams

GO FLY A KITE

If I was around when Ben Franklin said,
"New Jersey is like a barrel tapped at both ends"
I would have told him to "Go fly a kite!"
I like living in New Jersey
One of the original thirteen
They nicknamed the Garden State
And for all you people out there who say,
New Jersey is one big ugly turnpike
I say to you what I would have said to Big Ben
"Go fly a kite!"

MY FATHER

Biagio Cardelli, Born January 12, 1892

A Man of Many Dreams

HE BUILT WITH HIS HANDS

When my father came to this land he carried his tools in his hands
Tools to dig a new foundation in a "Nation, united, for which it stands"

Divided from his motherland,
He carried in His Heart the roots of his Family Tree
And planted them along with ninety million others to grow free without
fear
Tall as a redwood, to stand strong against the strain of gravity's pull
Small as the spruce, beckoning the wind,
To carry the rain clouds full of white snow
To roll under the sun with a thundering roar,
To break the icy stillness from the peaks above
To cool down the baked tablelands below

My father, an Indian from another world
A native stepping on a stone
To put another in place

"My Father Built With His Hands"
He believed in a nation for which it stands

Anthony Cardelli

A Better Man Than Me

My father was a better man than me
A better man than I would ever hope to be
With just a shovel he dug deep into the ground
And built a foundation for me to stand,
Against knee-level winds that keep trying to shake me down

The Pope

The Pope
That's my Pop
He never stops giving His Heart
Lending a hand when you have only one leg to stand on
Pulls you back up on your own two feet
With his foundation on his shoulders

My father came from across the sea.
To America and handed it to me
And what he left is still standing
But not by the likes of me

A Man of Many Dreams

MY OLD MAN

My old man
Carved castles in the sand
What a man, was My Old Man
Looking through the eyes of a two-year-old,
You'll know what I mean

My old man
Was always trying to explain to me
Looking through the eyes of a junior high,
You'll know what I mean

My old man
When I needed him the most,
Saw in my eyes how grown up I came to be

My old man
Is my father heaven on earth

My father before me
I will not forsake thee
For the power within me, left with what you have given me,
Shall lift the Family Tree a branch above
Toward the supreme height of life

My old man
Wore a checkered cap
Colors that snapped to any tie he chose

Anthony Cardelli

My old man
Had nothing to lose
He was a winner all the way

My old man
Used to say, "Rome was not built in a day"
But who's to say you can't give it a try

My old man
He was really something
Something that passes you by
And leaves you with a sigh
Why, oh why, did he have to die?

1st row center: My Father with co-workers

MY SISTER

1940's My sister Connie & Mom on Swan Street, Trenton NJ

1971 with my sister Connie at my niece Maryann's Wedding Day

Anthony Cardelli

MY SISTER WENT AWAY

My sister went away never to return
Leaving beautiful memories forever in my soul,
To keep the flame burning

Here today, gone tomorrow
No more time to spend or borrow
No one knows how far they will go,
On their journey through life on Trilogy Road

I pray each day and night,
For my prayers to rise high above the clouds
That my words will be inscribed,
On the peaks tinged with snow

OUT OF PLACE

My Sister lying unrest
Unsettled are the living she left behind
My Mother dressed in mourning
Keeping her in comfort
Lying out of place

A Man of Many Dreams

CONNIE: MY SISTER IS ON MY MIND

My Sister comes to mind
When I see a girl of nine,
Walking her baby brother of five home from school
Teaching him the traffic rules along the way

My Sister is in My Heart
A special part placed there from the start
To keep in time to the beat of life
My Sister, "God bless her soul"

1945 wearing our "Victory Shirts"
with my cousin Joey Telesca & my sister Connie

MY LOVE AND ROMANCE

Our Wedding Day August 25, 1954

A Man of Many Dreams

MY WIFE

I was right just once in My Life
And once is still enough for me
Each night before I go to sleep,
I add another day of living a beautiful life
To the day you became My Wife!

IN A SPECIAL PLACE

When I first saw you, you were too young to touch
As my eyes searched into your youth,
I felt all the beauty kept in store
Beyond our time
In a special place

In a special place
This side of Heaven
Between the Hudson and the Delaware,
God planted the seeds
And hammered golden stakes in the ground

Anthony Cardelli

My Anna

I can say it in a thousand words
Or break it down to one
Name her tune on the very first note
Because when I saw Anna,
That's all she wrote

She's pearl, emerald, and wheat
She's solid, shallow, and deep
She's precious, elegant, and sound
She's the best thing that has happened to me all around!

My Pearl

Time and time again,
I'm reminded of way back then
In better times when the world was my oyster,
With its shell full of pearls
Pouring out a steady rain of happy tears filtering through the air
When the world was my oyster
And you were "My Pearl"
All the silver and gold we left to the fishes in the sea
What we had was deeper than their shallow eyes could see!

Anthony Cardelli

SHE'S A DIAMOND IN THE ROUGH

She's a diamond in the rough
An emerald on the rocks
A precious pearl from the deep
Standing in the strength of golden wheat

She's my lady, she's my woman, she's my wife
The mother of my daughter, she's my life

She's the most important person in this world to me
She's the only one who keeps my sanity
She's one of a kind with the kind of beauty,
That makes me feel before my eyes let me see,
Before the rest of my senses, the sound, the scent and the taste,
Take over my body and mind, my heart and soul

THE COSMOS

At the break of dawn until the end of the day,
I follow the sun to lead me,
Into the twilight of the rising moon beaming on the star
Charting my way through endless space, "The Last Frontier"
Voices resounding over the Cosmos Galaxy
Floating me closer to your beautiful face!

"The Cosmos," that's what she means to me
Her smile, her laugh, every detail
From the smallest strand of her hair,
She takes with meticulous care

A Man of Many Dreams

THE SUN, THE MOON, AND THE STARS

You're the sun, the moon, and the stars
You're the three together
And you tell me exactly who you are

Although I never saw the sun rise
Never saw the moon glow
Or have I ever seen the stars shine

But the three together plus my feelings of the warmth from your embrace,
I feel the sun shining on your face
The stars sparkling in your eyes
And the glow from the moon beaming down to your face

I never saw the sun rise
I never saw the stars in your eyes
I never saw the moon beaming down on your face
But I feel its warmth from your embrace

Anthony Cardelli

UNTIL

Up until now
I never thought too much about anything
I never met anything head on
I would just roll with the punches to soften the blows
My favorite song was "Anything Goes"
I would never let anyone come close to where it hurt the most
Way down deep inside
Hiding on the dark side of the sun

ALIVE

I read about it, heard about it
Counted the ways with poets from the past
Took advice from the wise,
That the only thing permanent is change
Nothing really lasts
But after all the reading and listening to the words of the wise
The moment my eyes searched into your beauty,
I felt I was alive!

A Man of Many Dreams

IS YOURS, IS MINE

What's mine is yours
What's yours is mine
What a beautiful way to begin a lifetime
Meeting on the level
Parting on the square
All the wonderful years in between to share

What's yours is mine
What's mine is yours
From the beginning, until the end
Shall be for us to adore

FROM THE DAY WE VOWED

From the day we vowed to love, honor, and obey
Up until now, the wick of the candle that lighted,
The flame in our souls,
Still sticks to the light burning in "My Heart"
I still feel its warm tenderness from each newborn created
With the flavors we tasted from God's Hands
Sweeter than ever before

Anthony Cardelli

25TH ANNIVERSARY

I was right just once in my life, and once is still enough for me
Because after all these years that have floated by,
It's still clear sailing under sunny skies
And with only the stars to chart our way,
Over the moon shinning on the silver lining of Our Love
Yes, I was right just once in my life
On the night I told you that together we would celebrate
Our 25th anniversary!

A Man of Many Dreams

OUR FAITH IN THEE

You don't have to unmask
I know who you are
The stars in your eyes
Are lighting my way to Your Heart

You don't have to unmask to reveal it's you
I knew right away by the way you are glowing
You're sending vibrations, sparkling sensations
Through a string of cellos
With pleasure and quality, your speciality

You don't have to unmask to ask the question
For I know the answer to how lovely it would be
Unmasking together Our Faith in Thee

LOCKED IN MY HEART

I kept everything you gave me locked in My Heart
There's no way, no matter what you say or do
How can I forget what took a lifetime to collect
From the first smile you gave me
To your last cigarette
From the moment we met there was something I saw in your beauty,
That I have been searching for all My Life!

Anthony Cardelli

Beauty Is a Joy Forever

A thing of beauty is a joy forever
And I'm forever enjoying the beauty of you
You keep intact the five senses of my being
True, I was born with them
But I never made much use of them
There was something each one of them lacked

Now my eyes see clearly the beauty of your face
My ears hear the sound of your beautiful voice
My nose inhales the sweet scented fragrance your body expels
My mouth tastes the many delicious flavors of the love you impel
And with the slightest touch, I dwell into the feeling of life's endeavor
A thing of beauty is a joy forever!

A Man of Many Dreams

A SECOND CHANCE

If I was offered a second chance, I'd turn it down
I would never think of taking a chance of missing you,
On your turn around

If I was offered paradise,
The place only a fool would refuse to go, I wouldn't
For a fool I'd be in paradise without you

I don't need a second chance
I don't want a paradise
I need no special place, no particular time
I carry lightly the beauty I feel inside

Developing the negatives in the dark room of my mind
With each one hanging up to dry
To expose in front of my eyes for everyone to see
Through the smile on my face

Anthony Cardelli

THE MOMENT

The moment I looked into your eyes,
I felt the warmth of the sun
I felt all my yesterdays rolled into one
And as we focused into each other's view,
We knew that all our yesterdays were well worth living through
For in your eyes I found the star to chart our way to Paradise

ALL MY DEFENSES

I put up fences carefully
Planned all my defenses against the resistance of love
But you came along and with just the tip of your finger,
Knocked them all down in a row
And as each one fell My Heart felt lighter,
As I lifted from the ground with you in my arms!

A WINNER EVERY TIME

If I could hit the Pick-It,
Like I hit it with you,
I'd be a millionaire
And if I could cross the finish line,
Like I came across to you
I'd be a winner every time

A Man of Many Dreams

I Can't Get Next to Where You Are

There's something new that I can't get next to
Out there shinning brighter than a star
I felt a rush, but it swept right through me
I was so close and yet so far
I thought I found when you first came to me,
What I had lost was glowing in your eyes
But just as before, it rushed right through me
I can't get next to where your are

For all my yesterdays keep getting in my way
Leaving me with no place to put today
There's something new that I can't get next to
It's so close and yet so far
I see it in your eyes, tomorrow's brightest star!
I can't get next to where you are

In Your Eyes

In your eyes
I feel all I need to know
I didn't have to ask when something is wrong
Your eyes told me so
Even in the brightness of the sun,
I can see through the blinding sun,
A glow of amber fading in your eyes

Anthony Cardelli

AN OLD CLICHÉ

I still refuse to believe an old cliché I was told a long time ago
"The only thing permanent is change"
Let's bring back the better times we lived in
Before we fall completely out of it
Let's take a chance with romance
It worked once before in better times
Who's to say it won't anymore

We can recapture the wind
Blowing in the rapture we once knew
With time in our favor,
We can taste the flavors of our love
As fresh as the buds of Spring
And sprout our hearts in full bloom
For all the seasons of our love

BLIND DATE

I went on a blind date not knowing what was in store
A little less, a little more,
Crossed my mind as I walked up the front steps to knock on your door
When it opened I knew I was going to get more than I bargained for
For there standing in front of me was the beauty I thought I would never feel
My shallow eyes opened wide as I searched deep within
And under my breath in a silent whisper,
You listened to the sound of my inner feelings
Meeting you this day has made all my yesterdays well worth searching for

A Man of Many Dreams

A SIGHT FOR SORE EYES

You're a sight for sore eyesI haven't seen such beauty since we parted
But somehow in My Heart I felt we would meet
It feels so good to see such beauty again

You're a sight for sore eyes
I haven't seen such beauty since heaven knows when
Although time moved slowly in between
Seeing you now makes it all worthwhile

I always thought time to be unkind
But I take it all back
I was way out of line
For if it wasn't for time
Life would have no meaning, no rhythm, no rhyme

BURNING UP

Burning up alive in a storm
Without love, I can't keep warm
They say ignorance is bliss, but I've been kissed
And left a beautiful taste in my mouth

Burning up alive in a storm
With a kiss on fire
And cold tears dropping on my lips

Anthony Cardelli

DON'T BOTHER TO KNOCK

Don't bother to knock
My heart is always open for someone like you
Since the day you came into my view
I threw away the key
Just walk right in
Stay as long as you want to
Don't be afraid to take whatever you need
And if by chance it isn't there, don't despair
I always have a spare rolled up under my sleeve

CONFESSION

Everyone has a place they call home
A place to come back to no matter how far they may roam
You can travel the world and see for yourself,
All the riches and wealth it possesses
With all of its worth it wouldn't be enough,
To buy what you left back home on the shelf
And I ain't guessing 'cause . . .

I'm confessing that I love you
I cross my heart and I hope to die
I'll even make the sign of the cross
Which I should of made first to convince you
I didn't rehearse this confession that I'm making
It's a first for me but they say the first time it hurts,
So bad it's the best you'll ever feel
Confessing to you makes me feel that this is true
Like the kid who hollered fire
I'm burning with love for you!

A Man of Many Dreams

THE ONLY WAY TO GO

Whenever love comes on strong,
I love to meet it head-on
I never roll with the punches to soften the blows
It's the only way to go,
To know how it feels being knocked head over heels in love

EVEN IF

Even if I had known from the beginning,
It was all just a game,
It wouldn't have made a difference
I still would have fallen in love on the very first play
Because the moment we met I knew,
I couldn't play it any other way

HER KIND OF LOVE

Her kind of love
Makes me feel the warmth of the sun
On a cold rainy day
Her kind of love
Makes me feel through the darkness of the night
The glow of a star
Charting my way to dawn's early light

Anthony Cardelli

FIRST PLAY

Love is a no score in tennis and in certain other games
With nothing to lose and nothing to gain
But just like a fool I fell in love on the very first play
Even with knowing the rules,
I still wouldn't have played it any other way

In or out of doors love is a no score,
In tennis and in certain other games
It's never called in on account of darkness
And it's always left out in the rain after the game is over

In or out of doors, I feel I made the right move
To start you in motion to take notice,
That love is the only way to score

Love is a no score in certain games
Even if I knew you were playing a game,
I wouldn't have played it any other way
I still would have fallen in love
On the very First Play

A Man of Many Dreams

FOREVER YOURS

Love is charming, cozy, and warm
Soft and tender as a baby just born
An instant feeling, forever yours
But then again it can be a terrible bore
When played in a game when love is a no score

As long as my body has a mind,
There's no place no matter how near or far,
You'll never leave my sight
For when you came into My Open Heart
I locked you in and threw away the key

FORGIVING YOU

Forgiving you, I can easily do
But to forget what took a lifetime to collect,
I'm afraid will take another lifetime to do
For as long as this body has a mind,
There's no place on this earth I can go
Without your smile
The sound of your laughter
The many mornings after
The beautiful nights we fell asleep in each other's arms
Only to be awaken by nature's alarm,
To begin another delightful day
Filled with all the charm of God-Made Things

Anthony Cardelli

HERE'S A PENNY FOR YOUR THOUGHTS

I can recall when in better times,
I was the only one on your mind
And in Your Heart
Here's a penny for your thoughts

I can recall in better times,
My phone would ring right off the wall,
To get your message through
But lately, I don't know you at all
Here's a penny for your thoughts

I'd like to know what you're thinking
Although I love a mystery
But this one only you can solve
Here's a penny for your thoughts

It's been so long since you let me in
I felt the pain inside when your eyes were dry
With your tears dropping on the flame of your soul
Turning the burning coal in your heart to ashes
Here's a penny for your thoughts

So if you would be so kind, please satisfy my curiosity
And don't let me second-guess with my philosophy
Patience was always one of my faults
Here's a penny for your thoughts

A Man of Many Dreams

How Do I Love Thee

Love sets the stage with poets counting the ways
Composers in the back ground creating beautiful sounds
With lyrical expressions to the counting of the ways,
How do I love thee?
Let me count the ways of Elizabeth Browning
But, if I may, before I do,
Let me tell you in my own way

When I was a boy I saw love in my father's eyes,
Through my Mother's Heart
Now I am a man,
Feeling in your eyes, all the love in My Heart

Lady Luck

Lady Luck never ran out on me
She's my favorite charm
Wherever I go she always shows with her smiling face
Making me win every bet I place
You're my favorite
I saved you for last

Let's Make a Pitch

Let's all make a pitch and pick up the stitch,
We dropped in the ditch,
With the same needle and thread
Together we can re-knit the spread
To cover over all the flaws in the bed
To lay in peace and stand with settlement
Forever full in Body and Soul

Anthony Cardelli

IGNORANCE IS BLISS

How does it feel when you love someone?
How do you know when it's real?
Do you know right away?
Or does it happen, say, a minute or two later?
What if it never happens to you at all?
Can you live without it, never to feel its kiss?
Is it true what they say, "Ignorance is bliss"?
What you don't know, what you'll never have
You won't miss

I'LL NEVER BE OLD ENOUGH

I can tell when it's going to rain
I can feel it in my bones
I can tell when the sun is hiding behind the clouds
I can feel its rays slipping through
I'm old enough to predict the weather
But I guess I'll never be old enough,
To predict what a woman will do

THE WOMAN IN MY LIFE

The woman in my life
Keeps my sanity
Keeps my mind in reality
Keeps My Heart beating in time
To the rhythm of the present

The woman in my life
Keeps the past behind
And keeps the future right up front
For as her eyes search, the woman in my life
Keeps the flame in My Soul turned up on high
Burning alive in a storm

150

A Man of Many Dreams

THE CROSS WE BEAR

The woman in my life keeps the flame in My Soul burning bright
That sets my eyes a glow,
From the warm fire in My Heart
To let me feel life everlasting through each day and night
The woman in my life carries with me, the Cross We Bear

IMAGINATION

They say imagination isn't fact
But when I imagined what it would be like,
To spend and hour or so with you,
I was the lucky one out of the two of us
I lucked out when you walked into my life
You didn't bother to knock
Somehow you knew the door to my heart was left unlocked

OUR MUSIC

You just say the words that I've been longing to hear
Then with each happy tear that falls I will set to music,
For our hearts to beat as one
And as the world turns on a new day with or without the sun,
We will follow the sound of the beauty within
And let our music begin

Anthony Cardelli

IN THE BATTLE FOR LOVE

Although she has a double,
I have no trouble to set them apart
I feel it in My Heart
With or without her look-alike,
I can close my eyes and pick out her sound in a crowded place

Because
Just to hear her talk inspires me
And when I open my eyes
And see the smile on her face
And the way she walks
Is an inspiration to me

Although she's off limits,
I'd step out of bounds to throw my hat in the ring
And try to win her in the very first round
In the battle for love

A Man of Many Dreams

RIGHT ONE FOR ME

You were the right one for me,
I realize it now
What my shallow eyes never felt
I'm feeling now,
Just how deep your beauty runs

The woman in my life,
She's beautiful
Beautiful in more ways than one
The queen of the mermaids
That's how deep her beauty runs
She keeps My Soul burning all my sins

THE ONLY WAY TO SCORE

Love is a no score in tennis
And in certain other games
But just like a fool I fell in love on the very first play
Even with knowing the rules,
I still wouldn't have played it any other way

In or out of doors
I feel I made the right move to start you in motion
To take notice that love is the only way to score

Anthony Cardelli

LOVE IS A NO SCORE

If you don't want to get involved,
I think I got the problem solved
All that's needed is a racquet and a ball
And as long as we stay on the opposite sides of the net,
We can play all day out in the open,
Under the sun and continue at night under a flood of lights
Without the slightest notion of being bored
Because love is a no score in tennis,
And certain other games people play

GAMES

I don't play games
Love is the only way to score in the game I play
You don't hit and run on me without touching all the bases
I don't fool around; I play for keeps
Just the sound of a one-nighter gives me the creeps

Love was a no score in the game we called
How we played without it no one would believe
That we loved every minute of it, up until now

We've been rained on before
But when it rains it pours in the game we called
On account of darkness no longer can we see eye to eye,
Love's blinding light

A Man of Many Dreams

A Good Time

When was the last time you can recall we had a good time?
Was it the night we went to A. C., just you and me
And we stopped on the way for a glass of beer
In a special place called "The Blue Moon"
I was dressed after six; you were dressed before nine
And we entered into twilight time
We drove on toward our goal on lonely Route 206
I was a month past twenty-five holding your hand,
The night you turned twenty
Youth was all the money we needed
As we came out of our spell from the aroma of Absecon

Table for Two

Don't walk out on me
Because the moment you do
Loneliness will walk in
Before you close the door
Leaving me with all our yesterdays

I won't take more than a minute of your time
I know you're in a hurry to meet someone
Someone who grew tired of waiting
And left with someone else

That someone else told me to call you
And tell you when you open the door
I'll be there to escort you to the dining room
At a table for two
With lighted candles and wine

Anthony Cardelli

IT'S NOT EASY

It's not easy
For a man to understand,
The many changes a woman keeps going through
He never stops trying though
He keeps searching to feel how deep her beauty runs

For man knows a woman is beautiful in more ways than one
At first sight of her, a warm liking feeling sweeps over him
From the sun shining on her face
As tepid winds wave through her hair

At first sight, My Shallow Eyes
Caught just a glimpse of her beauty
But as my eyes searched I began to feel how deep it runs
She's beautiful, in more ways than one!

A Man of Many Dreams

JUST A ONE-NIGHT STAND

This wasn't part of the plan
Only was meant to be just a one-night stand
We both agreed no questions asked
No future, no past
Just a one-night stand
As long as it lasts

This wasn't suppose to happen
Wasn't on our mind
Just one night of candle light and wine
No talking in-between the lines

Holding hands across the table
Searching into each other's eyes
That's when all the plans fell apart
Because we both saw the same dream in our heart

Now we're looking at photographs,
Of what wasn't part of the plan
Wasn't meant to be
What a one-night stand created for you and me!

Anthony Cardelli

JUST AS I PREDICTED

In my first bout with love,
Love was the heavy favorite
The odds were a million to one
And the talk was I didn't stand a Chinaman's chance
But I went in swinging at the crack of the bell

And just as I predicted,
I got caught with a left hook I didn't see coming
It was so fast it came from nowhere
I was looking there was no way

And just as predicted
It was all over the first second I met love face to face
For at the sound of the bell, I went into a trance
And love cast a spell over me

JUST LIKE YOU WANT

Just like you want
The sun to keep shining through the rain clouds rolling by,
So do I

Just like you want
The moon tide to raise the ocean's floor,
With its beams dancing on the waves,
So do I

Just like you want
The stars to light up in the sky to chart the way,
So do I

Your wants are the same as mine
I can feel it in my bones
You don't want to live alone

A Man of Many Dreams

I ONCE WAS BLIND

I lost one of my senses a long time ago
It was heartbreaking for me to know
I would never be able to see the beauty of the future
In my darkness a beautiful light flashed through my eyes
And vibrated through my body
Just like that, I have my eyesight back
I can see how beautiful you are by the way you make me feel
I can see how beautiful you are, because you make me feel beautiful
I don't have to ask anyone
I feel it from the stars
And in my darkness, I feel the warmth of the sun smiling on your face, so fair,
And coolness from the moon, brushing your hair

Anthony Cardelli

YOUR HEART

If you give me your heart I'll handle it with care
For I know what's inside
I can see through your eyes how much love is in there

With all that love for me to share, I'll be beyond compare
Do everything, go anywhere the rest of my life with you
Holding my heart, too

NOTHING

What in the world would I do without you?
You're always near, when I need someone close
You're always here, when I need you the most
Only you can touch where I hurt the most

What in the world would I be without you?
Only you can see what never shows
Hidden deep inside from shallow eyes
What would I do? What would I be?
A two part question with just one word to answer
"Nothing"

A Man of Many Dreams

OUR GEMINI HEARTS

She's my Gemini Gal
I'm her Gemini Guy
We're just a couple of bows who tied the knot
Not too loose, not too tight

We're not saying we do everything right
But it's been so long since we did anything wrong
We don't need a penny for our thoughts
We know each other's faults
We see eye to eye
And can clearly read every word written in our mind

Although our bodies separate each day,
We carry each other in Our Hearts until twilight
With our star in sight once again,
We see each other in full view
And pour out the Love we stored up,
The hours we were apart
Over flowing all through the night
From the depths of Our Gemini Hearts

Anthony Cardelli

ONLY FOR YOUR EYES

Only for your eyes
The sun rises for you to follow you each day

Only for your eyes
The stars light up the night to chart your way
And the man on the moon beams a smile on his face
Only for your eyes

Only for your eyes
I'll show you the dream you made come true
The dream I gave up on when it became way overdue

THE TWO OF US

If it wasn't for the two of us,
The beauty that surrounds us now,
Would have never recaptured the rapture we feel
If it wasn't for the two of us,
Our eyes would be searching in vain
Even from a bird's-eye view

A Man of Many Dreams

It Was Always Anna

It's always been you
There never was anyone else
From the first day I caught sight of you
The magnet of love drew you closer to My Heart

The one I love isn't a friend of mine
It happened so fast we didn't take the time
We fell in love the moment we met
There wasn't time to be friends

What we had in mind was to begin something that never will end
There were times when knee level winds blew us out of bounds
But Our Love held fast and together we buckled down
And weathered the storm
Standing once again on solid ground

Anthony Cardelli

It's Great to Be Alive

I was once very happy everything was going my way. I was full of life with my work and play. I was a winner every morning when I opened my eyes and felt the warmth of your body close to mine. After we showered and with a full breakfast under my belt, we parted with a kiss, and I was ready for my day of collecting my pits from the traps I had set. Call my local bookie and place my bets, meet you for lunch, and with a cocktail or two, talk over our plans for the evening to come. Then took a ride in our open convertible under the sun. The air was refreshing, filtering through our lungs and filling our heads with mid-afternoon dreams. Then we came upon a beautiful spot and decided to stop, laying a blanket under a weeping willow. We gathered some leaves for our pillow and fell into a deep sleep to the sounds of nature playing overtures of spring. We slept through the whole score, only to be awakened by the sound of Mr. Frog, who hit a bad cord. We got up and stretched our bodies and realized Father Time had ticked pass five. We looked at each other, and with a smile, we easily read what didn't have to be said.

"It's great to be alive"!

A Man of Many Dreams

GIFT OF TIME

From the darkroom of my mind,
I began developing negatives that never caught the camera's eye
Photographs of you kept flashing in clear view,
Of the beauty I left behind

The pleasures of past treasures of your company vibrated through me
Seeing the moon glowing on your face
And the warmth from the sun when we embraced
The fresh scented fragrance that filled the air,
From the wind brushing your hair
And with a smile that broke the silence around me
From the happy tears dropping from my eyes
Composing a sound of musical notes blending with the season,
As I listen to you speak words with reason

Although you are gone, you'll always be near
For one never loses, as long as one remembers
The precious gift of time we spent through the years

Written sometime after July 15, 1991

LOST LOVE

Anthony Cardelli

Vows

What ever happened to the vows we made?
To Love, Honor, and Obey
Were they just words spoken in ceremony?
By two people acting out a play
What ever happened to the vows we made
On Our Wedding Day?

A Home to Leave Behind

Whatever happened to the vows we made?
We promised to keep locked in the heart,
We said would never break
I never dreamed it would end this way
My dreams were so beautifully arranged,
To the setting of our wedding day

But I would only be kidding myself if I were to say,
I never believed in the only thing permanent is change
Life in itself dwells in its shell between heaven and hell
To pick a place and build a home to leave behind

A Man of Many Dreams

A House Full of Love

A house full of love
Overflowing in every room
Poured down the drain
When she called the game on account of rain

In better times life was peaches & cream
We took the bitter with the sweet
And mixed them with the flavors of Our Love

We used to be such good friends
A friendship we vowed would never end
Every game we played in or out of doors
Only one rule was set as in tennis,
Love was a no score
But we can only stay for so long
Before it starts to get boring

A house was once full of love
Overflowing in every room
Got caught up in the middle of a storm,
Of heavy gales and drowning rain
Pouring all the love down the drain

We used to be such good friends
An infinite pair
An unlimited sign
We put up everything we had
Without limits of time

Anthony Cardelli

To Love, to Honor, & Obey

I would like to repeat the vows I made to you
On Our Wedding Day
To Love, To Honor, & Obey
And may I add with the promise to make them stick
With no tricks up my sleeve
I ran all my bluffs out of town
I blew them into the wind

She left me flatfooted
With knee-level winds coming from behind
Caught me in the back
Flipped me head over heels

All My Soul, My Heart

I gave you all My Soul, My Heart
All the parts in between right from the start
I left nothing out
I gave you everything
Now after all these years, without shedding one tear,
You're telling me it wasn't enough
The pain I felt from your opening line,
Punched a hole into the emptiness you left me behind

A Man of Many Dreams

BEHIND THE SMILE

After all the years that have pasted by
I still feel the pain when someone in the crowd mentions your name
They don't see the tears I keep holding back inside
I drown out the sound with a good hearty laugh
And ask a foolish question, "Who in the hell is that?"
But they know all to well what is really on my mind
They can read between the lines
I can never hide from the smile on my face

SOME OTHER BIRD

Is it true what I heard?
You've been nesting with some other bird
When you fly away from our Family Tree
Then you can spread the word from vine to vine
Don't waste your time flying back to me

If it's true what I heard
That you're nesting up a tree with some other bird
Don't mess with me

There's word going around from vine to vine
That you're two-timing on the double
And that spells trouble with a capital T
'Cause if it's true,
Don't mess with me

Don't expect me to be under your lock and key
While you're flying around fancy-free
'Cause your philosophy is ancient history

Anthony Cardelli

A Perfect Heart

We met on the level and parted on the square,
Going our separate ways
Each carrying a cross to bear
With concentration divided we decided without hesitation,
To make the break and piece together all the good parts
To make a perfect heart

Broken Heart

I know I'm not alone being left with a broken heart
But I don't want to fall in line with all the rest
Waiting for someone with the spare parts to start it beating again
So, I'll do it myself because I'm not going to be left on the shelf
I wished, I hoped, I also prayed for the day,
You would say those words that would mend this broken heart
No other would know where to start
You, only you, know where to pick up all the shattered pieces to mend
my heart

A Man of Many Dreams

IN THE DARKROOM OF MY MIND

In the darkroom of my mind
Negatives that never caught the camera's eye,
Develop positive prints of all the beauty I left behind
And I feel as my eyes search back into past photographs,
All the beauty I missed

How can I forget what took a lifetime to collect?
Starting from the very first moment we met
I caught the first two happy tears
Before they dropped from my eyes
And let them fall back inside
Hidden from the sun, never to dry

How can I forget what took a lifetime to develop?
Negatives of all the wonderful times that were spent
Are kept in the darkroom of my mind
Negatives that never caught the camera's eye
Are still hanging up to dry

Anthony Cardelli

OUT OF SIGHT, OUT OF MIND
(IS THERE SUCH A PLACE)

I just can't forget what took a lifetime to collect
The smile on your face
The sound of your beautiful voice rings softly in my ear
And the sweet scented fragrance that filters through the air,
Brushes upon my lips the flavors of Your Love

What fools we mortals be
To never feel the beauty in God-Made Things
Our eyes are too shallow to see
We never listen to the sound

It was easy for me to leave behind,
Photographs, tables and chairs, arts and crafts
And all other material things we shared
But, I have yet to find a place in this world,
Called out of sight, out of mind

Out of sight, out of mind,
Is a place I've been trying to find,
Ever since you left me behind,
Your face is in front of me everywhere I go

I must have covered every inch of dirt on this earth
From Istanbul to Timbuktu
But I've reached an age where time can't heal
Thinking of you

A Man of Many Dreams

FOUR SEASONS OF OUR LOVE

Our love started to grow with the fresh buds of Spring
Spouting in full bloom in the middle of Summer
Only to wilt in the Fall
And die in the cold of Winter

In the four seasons of our love
We tasted the sweet flavors of Spring and Summer
And the bitterness of Fall and Winter

Two people meet and fall in love
Make promises they'll never keep
Living in between on fantasies and dreams
That falls apart at the seams
Then live out the rest of their lives in a false reality

When you don't get what you want
Heaven help who you get!

Anthony Cardelli

FROM NOW ON

I thought I had a friend
One that I could trust
A person who would listen,
When I just needed to talk
Knowing I didn't want any answers

From now on
It can never be the way it was
We can never pick up where we left off
We lost the one thing that was free
The "love" between you and me

From now on
We can never touch without hurting
The pain would be too much to bear

From now on
It can never be
That's the price a one-time loser pays

From now on
It can never be the way it was
But I can never forget,
What took a lifetime to collect

A Man of Many Dreams

HEART FOR RENT

I'm putting up My Heart for rent
My love broke the lease when she met her Hercules
Who wrapped the Golden Fleece around her
And flew the coup and left me flatfooted to regroup

You can rent My Heart week to week
Or by the month to play it safe and keep the peace
No more long-term lease
It's still in good shape; there's a lot of love left to share
She broke it but I saved up enough parts to spare

I'M RUNNING A SALE TODAY

I'm running a sale today,
On a broken heart
I'm practically giving it away
All it needs is a few spare parts,
To start it beating on time again
I won't try to pull the wool over your eyes
It's been battered, bruised, and used

I'm running a sale today,
On a broken heart
It's been battered, bruised, and overused
But if you can find the right fuse and a few spare parts,
It will start beating again just like new

Anthony Cardelli

ALL MY EGGS

When I first fell in love I felt it never would end
I thought this feeling would last as long as the sun,
Shining brightly inside me

With invisible rays to guide me through the day into the night
From the glow of the moon,
Lighting up the stars to sparkle in my eyes

I don't have much to offer
But you're welcome to what's left
Before you came along I gave most of it away
I gambled and lost on my first bet with love
I put up all my eggs in one basket
And after she left I was lucky to be left with just a few

A Man of Many Dreams

NEVER FALLS ON ME

It falls from the skies
Slips through the clouds
Drops in the trees
Runs along its branches
From there, I don't know where
Because it never falls on me

ON THE WINGS OF A DOVE

I gambled and lost in the game of love
I put up all I had on the wings of a dove
There for a while I was riding high on just a smile
Floating on a cloud with stars in my eyes
Until the dove turned into a hawk

TIME TO DECIDE

I think it's time for you to decide
And when you do, you don't have to tell me
Because all I have to do is look in your eyes
And see the tears filling up
Ready to fall slowly down your face
Drowning my hopeful thoughts

Anthony Cardelli

A LONG TIME IN BETWEEN DRINKS

It's been a long time in between drinks
A long time since I've tasted the sweet flavors of love
A long time since I've felt the warmth of the sun on a cold rainy day
When love would transcend loneliness into a beautiful feeling,
As it faded away

It's been a long time in between drinks
A long time since my eyes searched into the beauty of the naked trees
Evergreens fully dressed
Tall timbers standing against knee-level winds
Too proud to bend

It's been a long time since I felt the warmth of the sun,
On a cold rainy day
That's how she used to make me feel before she went away

It's been a long time in between drinks
A long time since I've tasted the sweet flavors of her love
A recipe only she could mix
That would pour instant happiness upon my lips

A Man of Many Dreams

YOU DON'T HAVE TO TELL ME

You don't have to tell me
I see what you're about to say
It's written all over your face,
What I already read through your eyes
I felt all the emptiness
Way down deep inside where it hurts
The place you always get to first,
With tenderness and care
The pain rises over my head,
With all its energy to inherit the wind

I'LL FORGIVE YOU

I'll forgive you as long as I remember
For I'll never forget what has taken a lifetime to collect
The memories are well-kept negatives,
I keep stored in the darkroom of my mind

No matter how far I travel positive prints develop in front of me,
Showing the love I left behind

I've tried out of sight, out of mind
Waited to heal with the grace of time
But photographs of you kept flashing in my view
Time sometimes can be rude and by-pass open wounds

Anthony Cardelli

I Vowed

I couldn't wait to ask you until Monday,
What time I could call
That's why I'm calling you now after half past ten
To end this feeling I vowed never to start again

I vowed never to start again
What had ended along time ago,
When I lost my first love
I searched for a while but all was in vain
The love I lost,
I would never feel the same

In Clear View

When you told me we were through,
Anyone I tried to tell already knew
The pain became stronger finding out,
I was the last to know

I took some advice from a doctor of love
And went to a place far out of your sight
When I got there I became aware,
That I was just wasting my time

Right in front of me in clear view,
Photographs of you kept developing,
From the darkroom of my mind
As far away as Timbuktu

A Man of Many Dreams

IT WOULDN'T BE EASY

I knew it wouldn't be easy
But then again, I never dreamed it would be this hard
Forgiving you caused some pain
But it wasn't strong enough to last

I went through it without much sweat or strain
But trying to forget what took a lifetime to collect
I'm afraid time isn't helping at all
In fact it's adding to the stress and pain

Because no matter how near or far I get,
To get away from the sight of you,
The negatives that never caught the camera's eye,
I carried in the darkroom of my mind, hanging up to dry
And the swollen tears filling my eyes
Developing in clear view out in the open sun,
Positive prints of all the beauty I left behind

Anthony Cardelli

WHO KNOWS BETTER THAN I

Who knows better than I?
I can see the tears that never fall out of your eyes
I can tell by the sound of your laughter
When you're crying inside
I can taste the bitterness upon my lips

I can feel the pain from the tears you keep holding back,
Behind that certain smile
And feel the pain of loneliness as I read between the lines
The words you keep hidden in the darkroom of your mind
Who knows you better than I?
I can sense when we're in a crowed place
By the look on your face your somewhere in time
Drifting out in space

Who knows you better than I
When you feel trapped and want to be set free?
I just open my heart
And let you walk out on me

A Man of Many Dreams

WITH JUST ONE WORD

I gambled and lost everything that I possessed,
With my very first bet on love
I thought the odds were in my favor
So I put up all I had
With Lady Luck standing beside me, I could do no wrong

You can make it happen with just one word
To start the ball rolling
Off the moss growing under my shoes
Just one word; that's all it will cost
Not a penny lost

You can make it happen with just one word
You can turn it all around,
With just a singular one syllable sound
By answering Yes

The best in me will come out on top
You'll have the pick of the crop in a golden harvest
We'll nest the rest of our lives
With just one word, Yes!

Anthony Cardelli

MOOD INDIGO

It's a blue world without you
Turning on the dark side of the sun
Where it never turns dark enough to see the stars
Never sets a glow in the twilight
It's an emptiness filled with broken dreams
No sea, no sky, no clouds drifting by
No rainbows, no end to the mystery of my love and I
It's a blue world alone in a mood indigo
Without you

You ain't been blue no, no, no
You ain't never been blue, 'til you have that mood indigo
That feeling that goes sticking right down to your shoes

You ain't been blue no, no, no
I always get that mood indigo when my baby breaks with me
I always get that mood indigo when one and two don't make three
'Cause, I don't want anyone else to share the apple we turned into a pair
I'm not the type to put up a fight

A Man of Many Dreams

RECAPTURE THE RAPTURE

I saved a lot of things from the past
That are worth a thousand times more today
But what good would it do to sell them,
When the one thing I should of held on to,
I let slip through my fingers and fall out in space
Feeling the lost now that it's too late,
To recapture the rapture of your embrace

To recapture the rapture I once knew,
Is the cost I must pay until the final toll
Saddest words written,
Saddest words spoken from tongue and pen

YOU DON'T HAVE TO TELL ME

You don't have to tell me
I see what you're about to say
It's written all over your face,
What I already read through your eyes
I felt all the emptiness
Way down deep inside where it hurts
The place you always get to first,
With tenderness and care
The pain rises over my head,
With all its energy to inherit the wind

Anthony Cardelli

SITTING IN A BAR

Sitting in a bar
Surrounded with unfamiliar faces
Drowning my sorrows in my beer,
Where it all began
And as my eyes search in the past,
Photographs flashed through my mind
Scenes of fantasies and dreams that never came true
Precious cargo I didn't handle with care,
Got lost somewhere and was carried out to sea

COLLECTIVE MEMORIES

I know sending flowers on the hour,
Would be overdoing it, it's true
But it was a beautiful way to get the message through
It worked once before
Who's to say it won't anymore

I'm ready to take a chance on romance once again
I tried out of sight, out of mind
And found I was just wasting my time,
Seeing you there right in front of my eyes
Because everyplace I went,
Collective memories of you, I carried deep inside

A Man of Many Dreams

TALKING TO MYSELF

I keep talking to myself
Asking what went wrong
Talking to myself what brought it on
But like everything else nothing really lasts
And tell myself this too shall pass

For the only thing permanent is change
And with Father Time on my side,
I'll adjust and rearrange
Go someplace out of sight, out of mind
Leaving all the memories of you behind

THE LOVE I LEFT BEHIND

Lost love found same
In the middle of nowhere
The last place I thought I would find,
The love I left behind
But, there it was right in front of me
All the things I tried to put out of sight, out of mind
I guess I'll never forget what took a lifetime to collect
The laugh, the heart, the soul
Every detail, to the smallest strand of your hair
I can't stop comparing, no matter where I go
Whether it be around the corner or as far as Timbuktu
I've reached an age to where all the beauty in the world
Reminds me of you

Anthony Cardelli

The Memories of You

All my yesterdays keep getting in the way
Because I have yet to find a place in this world,
Far enough out of sight, out of mind
No matter where I go
Whether it be around the corner or Timbuktu
I can't forget what took a lifetime to collect
The memories of you

Two People

Two people meet and fall in love
They make promises they'll never keep
They live in between fantasies and dreams
Unaware they'll never come true
Or fall apart at the seams

They Just Won't Go Away

They just won't go away
They keep getting in the way
Each day is the same
Whoever said the only thing permanent is change,
Never had a bunch of yesterdays falling in front of today

They just won't go away
They keep getting in my way
Each day is the same as the next
'Cause all my yesterdays keep getting in front of tomorrow

They just don't make them like you anymore
They broke the mold
Dug a hole and buried it deep

A Man of Many Dreams

NICE GUYS FINISH FIRST

I gambled and lost so many times before
So what's the big deal losing once more?
I'm running true to form
My past performance shows
I never place a bet to win right on the nose
And every time I cross the finish line,
There's no one tailing behind

But I never thought I would run dead last with you
And loved every minute of it, too, for letting me know,
That nice guys finish first with you
Since then, I've canceled all bets
I feel so far ahead of life after death

THIS RAINY DAY

Just like a fool, I didn't save for this rainy day
It never crossed my mind you would leave me behind
Under a sky full of clouded memories
Way back then the sun was always on time
I would follow it every which way
Never would I lose sight of you
Feeling its warmth into early twilight
And when it disappeared the moon would glow on the stars
To chart my way to our own little paradise we once knew

Anthony Cardelli

TIME, THE TATTLETALE

Out of sight, out of mind
And with the grace of time is the best place to be,
To set one free of all ties of the past,
I was told by people in the know
But such a place I have yet to find
Because no matter where I've been,
The memories of you I can't leave behind
The distance didn't matter
I have reached an age of everyone I meet,
Reminds me of the latter

For as long as this body has a mind,
Old Father Time will keep flashing back
To the beauty that once was yours and mine

Out of sight, out of mind
Used to work for me every time
But with you it didn't somehow
You kept appearing in the oddest places
I couldn't get your face out of my mind,
Anywhere, anyplace, anytime
Photographs of you develop right in front of my view
From the negatives I forgot to leave behind

A Man of Many Dreams

TRAVELING ON A METRO LINER

Traveling on a Metro Liner
Sipping champagne
Railing down the Carolinas to play in a game
With a set of rules that equally applies,
To in or out of doors

Love is a no score
In tennis and in certain other games
It's only called on account of darkness
And always left out in the rain

Only fools fall in love on the very first play
For they take all the fun out of the game
And spend the rest of their lives loving in vain

Knowing all the rules of the game we were playing
Especially the one we wholeheartedly agreed upon,
I knew My Heart would fall on the very first play
I can't play that game anymore,
With Love as a no score

Anthony Cardelli

WAITING FOR THE TIDE

What's happening to me happens to people,
Who didn't prepare to prevent
I saw it coming but my foundation wasn't strong enough,
To hold back the cascading waters,
That cracked through the walls of my resistance

Now, everything I possess is running downstream
Drowning all my hopes and dreams deep under the sea
Leaving on a dry dock, knowing the tide will never come in

Sitting on a dock high and dry
Waiting for the tide to rise for my ship to come in
But the undertow keeps pulling her further out to sea
All my hopes and dreams she carries on her deck,
Are blowing overboard in the cold waters
Frozen from the winds into icebergs

A Man of Many Dreams

WELL WISHES OF THE PAST

I got some bad news today
But that's okay
I've been handicapped before
And had to play it under par

I lost the sight from my eyes
The sound never to hear
The smell I'll never taste
To feel inside no longer pours out of me,
The love you stopped pouring in

I never stop the flow of love
What's mine is yours to the last drop
All the love you keep pouring in could fill an ocean
And all the rivers that flow
Running through streams to fill in the lakes
To where the water falls into a fountain full of coins
From well wishes of the past

Anthony Cardelli

WHEN I LOST YOUR LOVE

When I lost your love,
I lost the beauty in my life
From that moment on my world was without a song
No longer would I touch the softness of your face
Or feel the warmth from your embrace

Yes, when I lost your love, I lost all of my senses
I was uneasy, slowly going out of my mind
Staying out of your sight

I would keep busy during the day
But oh! Those lonely nights of sitting home
Thinking to myself with the negatives in the darkroom of my mind
Kept developing positive prints of the photographs I left behind
When at that time I thought would keep me from seeing you

A Man of Many Dreams

WHERE THE SUN NEVER SHINES

I fell in love just once
And once is good enough for me
At first I felt its charm, its tenderness and warmth
Happy tears I cried each day out in the open sun
Only to feel each drop drying up one by one
The world was my oyster and I dwelled in its shell
But then all hell broke loose
Causing my tears to fall back inside
Way down deep where it hurts the most
A place the sun never comes close

For when it rains, it pours
Flooding over the pain
Time will never heal in a place,
Where the sun never shines when it rains

WHIRLPOOL OF SADNESS

My way of life is easy to bare
Ever since you told me how much you care
Let no tears drop from your eyes,
Into a whirlpool of sadness
For when ever you cry, I wish you happy tears
Since the day you left me the teardrops began to fall,
Into a whirlpool of sadness cascading in

Anthony Cardelli

THE LOST LOVE I FOUND

When I lost my first love,
I felt I would never feel the same
But as my eyes searched into its beauty,
I began to feel its warmth rising from way down deep inside me
Lighting the flame to burn desire into My Soul
And glow through my eyes to show once more, the lost love I found
As my eyes searched its beauty and felt you close

SIXTH SENSE

My eyes can't see you
But I know how beautiful you are
For into my life you came
Lighting the flame in my soul
Feeling the warmth from the sun with your embrace
Feeling the sparkling sensation through your eyes
And feeling the glow of the moon framing your face

WHAT ARE YOU LOOKING AT?

"What are you looking at?" she would ask
I'm looking at someone that no one in the world would see,
Would feel, would hear, would inhale, would taste.
Your eyes, your smile, your lips, your nose,
The clothes you wear go together wherever you travel
Through all the ups and downs, it was great to have you around
As soon as my eyes open to begin another day,
You're near and appear here and there in the atmosphere

Written sometime after July 15, 1991

A Man of Many Dreams

WITHOUT YOU

When you're the last one to know
It hurts too much to show
What you thought you won
You lost long ago
The first thing that comes to mind,
Is when you begin to retrack your thoughts
To where you overtrained
You stop at all the stations, one by one you revisited
But they're not the same
Without you

YOU CAN MAKE IT HAPPEN

You can make it happen
With just one word
You can turn it all around
With a singular sound

You can make it happen
With just a sigh
It's not a matter of life or death
But if you just say the word, Yes
I'll start living instead of just waiting to die

Anthony Cardelli

ME WITHOUT YOU

Me without you
I hate to think of what I would be without you
Next to nothing I was before I met you

But me without you now,
I would be a body without a Soul
Never finding peace of mind
With a Heart filling up with sad tears falling back from my eyes
Leaving me standing catatonic against the four seasonal winds,
That would never change the nothing that was frozen into place

Me without you
I never dreamed I'd be without you
You were always the star stealing every scene
Good or bad you had a way to make me forget,
About all my other dreams that were overdue

Me without you
I stopped dreaming the day I met you
And started building my world around the dreams,
You turned into reality
Starting with a house on a hill surrounded with trees
Rich with fruit and leaves
A garden of splendor
With a fresh scented fragrance filtering through the air
Tasting the flavors of Our Love
Filling up in every room

You made My Favorite Dream come true
On the first day I met you!

MY GREATEST DISCOVERY

My greatest discovery was my greatest loss.

I miss my wife, miss the life we had

I miss the warm feeling of the love we shared
I miss her tender loving care, her smile,
Her laughter to the smallest strand of hair
I miss the aroma of love that awakens me from a deep sleep
From the endless mornings of her body next to mine
Beginning the day with passion that lasted throughout the morning,
Afternoon, and evening
I miss the conversations, the walks together, the family picnics,
The holidays, the trips to faraway places, the disagreements, the makeups . . .

LETTERS TO ANNA

Written after July 15, 1991

A Man of Many Dreams

MY HEART

Anna,

"My Heart" is heavy to lighten it. I wake up each morning and think about one of the many good times we had together. It helps me get through the day.

I miss you Anna, the laugh, the "Heart", the "Soul", to the smallest strand of hair, the tender loving care, the look of love, the smile, your courage, when it was time to leave. You were strong when I weakened, when I was betraying myself. You never gave up on the guy you wanted to grow old with.

I love you Anna for making me feel as you were departing, that I would be strong and take care of "Our Family". Anthony, Elizabeth and DeAnna are beautiful as the day you left. Cathy is you, she's strong and beautiful. Jeppy found peace and doing great and is giving all he's got and then some.

Love,
Hop

Written 1995

Anthony Cardelli

Knowing Me

Anna,

It's never easy for me to say I miss you . . . I really do.
I miss the life we shared. I miss the tender loving care, the warm feeling of being in love. I miss the scent, the talks, the walks along the beach at sunrise and twilight. Dining as the sun sets over the bay. Out of the four seasons, summer was our favorite. Anna, it was and still is you, always you. What's real to me is Cathy and the children and little Miss Gianna Marie, the rest of my life is false. I've known you since I was twenty. Sixty years have passed. I see you and remember in my heart. When I look at your great-granddaughter, I see you.

Love,
Hop

Written June 2009

A Man of Many Dreams

JUST BEFORE SUNRISE

Dear Anna,

You left this world just before sunrise, July 15, 1991. Nineteen years have past. Your daughter will be fifty-five, your grandson, Anthony is thirty-three, Elizabeth thirty-two and DeAnna is thirty. Each one made the usual mistakes. The part of growing up is learning to correct the mistakes after, not before. Cathy took the reins and led them through the bad times and pulled up from a gallop to a trot into the good times. Anthony was first to marry.

Christmas was celebrated, but not like when we were altogether. Cathy kept the traditions you created and she still to this day, every September, she and your grand-daughters jar tomatoes. Thanksgiving and Christmas, she prepares enough dishes to feed an army. Christmas week she bakes cookies, the girls help and this year your great-grandchild, Gianna Marie was helping with her Aunt Lizzy and Aunt Dee Dee. She is going to have company before this February 14th, a baby brother, Anthony and Jillian are christening him, Joseph. Anna, Gianna Marie is you all over again—your baby photograph, I just can't stop looking at her. I hope I live long enough to hear her say, "what are you looking at G.G. Pop"? That's what she calls me G.G. Pop. Anna, I feel in my heart and soul that you are near us in spirit. I believe you are with us and that's why everything that we have is because of you. Anthony's happy, Elizabeth, happily married and DeAnna's future looks bright. She met someone and maybe she'll find her happiness. I read once that happiness makes up in life what it lacks in length. We've been through many sad times that seem to never end. You can be happy for just one day and it clears the air of ill winds.

Love,
Hop

Written January 2010

Anthony Cardelli

Being In This World with Me

Anna,

I love you for being in this world with me
I love you for being in the right place, at the right time
For when I think of how long it took for us to meet,
The odds were One Million B.C.,
To Nineteen-Fifty-Three or Four
I couldn't ask for more!

I love you for being in this world with me

Hop

MY DAUGHTER

Catherine Ann Cardelli Ciccia

Anthony Cardelli

I Met a Girl

I met a girl along time ago
It was in the Spring
And I watched her grow more beautiful each day
As tepid winds brushed through her hair
While she blossomed with the colors of Summer green and pastels

She

She's a stick out in a crowd
Proud as a peacock
Standing there with her beautiful blonde hair framing her face
Nature painted with special care

Dipping her brush into the Cosmos
She dabbed two crystal blue stars to sparkle in her eyes
Rapped a rainbow around her hand and swirled it,
Until it turned into rosy red to brush on her cheeks

Anthony Cardelli

NOT JUST ANOTHER PRETTY FACE

To everyone else she's just a pretty face
Just another one among the many pretty girls all over the place
But to me she's all of them rapped in one and then some
Only heaven knows how deep her beauty runs
For surely heaven is where she was sent from
With her golden hair and emerald green eyes

CLASS OF THE FIELDS

You're the class of the fields
You stand out in the crowd
Just to be in your company makes me feel proud
You give more than you take
Care for the sake of others
People profit from you more than they would allow

A Man of Many Dreams

Elegance

She's the elegance of emerald green
Her beauty runs deeper than precious pearls
And on the surface the strength of her splendor,
Is seeded and sowed in a harvest of golden wheat

Anthony Cardelli

I Was There When It Happened

I was there when it happened
I saw two people fall in love
I listened to the vows they made on their wedding day
Inhaling with each word,
To love, to cherish, to honor and obey
The smell of burning wax from the lighted candles, melting their hearts

To taste the flavors of love pouring on each other's lips
And sealed it with a kiss
I was there when it happened
Two people feeling eternal bliss!

Catherine & Giuseppe's Wedding Day, November 14, 1976

A Man of Many Dreams

HAPPY TEARS

I've been asked to sing for the bride & groom,
Without any music in this loved-filled room
A love that Cathy & Joe have built through the years
So, I would like to pick out some lyrics
And drop some notes on the happy tears
That are flowing on this special day

So, if you'll bear with me without the strings of "Costa"
Without the swinging of Basie
And without the rhythm of Riddle
I'll try to capture them all in my mind
And take you back a few years in time

Anthony Cardelli

THE DAUGHTER OF MY PEOPLE: OUR FAMILY TREE

Through DeAnna, Elizabeth Ann and Anthony
"The Daughter of My People"
How grateful and proud thou art of thee,
To see the future growth of Our Family Tree,
Through Elizabeth Ann and Anthony
Is the most precious gift given to me!

Catherine Ann Cardelli-Ciccia
"The Daughter of My Future People"
I thank you for letting me see before I leave,
The added branches of Our Family Tree

Elizabeth, DeAnna and Anthony had assured me from the fear of when
I leave,
They will be near and you will never be alone

God Bless You,
Daddy

Just Once in My Life

I was right just once in my life
And that one time sticks in my mind
No matter where I go
I never leave it behind or toss it aside
It leads with me through my eyes
Feeling all the beauty I knew I would
As I am now feeling

Way back then, being right
That one time in my life
Feeling beyond my time and place
When I saw Your Beautiful Face,
Framing Our Family Tree

Yes, being right once is more than enough for me
You're beautiful in more ways than one
Beauty surrounds you with children on a Carousel
You'll never walk alone!

Anthony Cardelli

From the Womb

After forty-eight years the most precious pearl in the world
Washed ashore from the pounding surf
It slept under the sea a hundred fathoms deep
Only to be awaken by a deliverer's hands
From the womb of,
"The Daughter of My People"!

Written the day my grandson Anthony was born, May 12, 1977

MY GRANDCHILDREN

Anthony, Elizabeth & DeAnna

Anthony Cardelli

A Beautiful Story to Be Told: My Family Tree

The Daughter of My People
Was born to carry three branches to grow My Family Tree
DeAnna, Elizabeth Ann, and Anthony

DeAnna came sooner than expected, although she was last
And Elizabeth Ann was in such a rush,
Her heart skipped a beat and finished second
And Anthony, he came out nice and neat
And got spoiled being first

God blessed them one by one
And filled their hearts with love to be loved
Two precious pearls, "That's my girls"
A golden harvest of wheat, "That's my boy"

A rainbow of silver and gold
A treasure of precious metals arched across the sky
Melting under the sun
Pouring into everyone's hearts
To give the body's soul
A beautiful story to be told!

A Man of Many Dreams

BURSTING WITH PRIDE:
MAY 12, 1977

I feel like I'm dancing on a cloud!
Proud as a peacock standing tall in a crowd!
Bursting with joy!
I just became a grandfather to a baby boy!
After forty-eight long years, he's got me crying happy tears,
For making me see the future of Our Family Tree!

I'm bursting with pride, bursting with joy!
I just became the grandfather of a baby boy!
He tipped the scales, I'm bursting with pride, bursting with joy!
I just became "Pop Pop!"
The proud Pop Pop of a baby boy!

You're the class of the field!
You're my Triple Crown!
You stick out in a crowd!
My Blue Chip Stock!
I'm as proud as a peacock
With my head way above the ground!

I'm bursting with pride, bursting with joy!
I just became the grandfather of a baby boy!
So have a cigar, and Joe, set 'em up around the bar
Until last call for all!

219

Anthony Cardelli

Wrapped in a Rainbow Towel

My grandson
He's beautiful, beautiful in more ways than one
Heaven only knows, how deep his beauty runs
For heaven is where he was sent from!

Wrapped in a rainbow towel
The sun followed him down
Floating on a snow white cloud
With a chorus of Guardian Angels singing in the background
To the resounding voice of the Great Spirit!

Under a galaxy of crystal blue stars
Charting the way from a heavenly place
With the moon beaming down on his face
My grandson, he's beautiful,
Beautiful in more ways than one!

Antonino Giuseppe Ciccia

A Man of Many Dreams

Beautiful in More Ways Than One

If I were to describe all the beauty I see,
Every time I look into his eyes,
It would take me a lifetime, and then some
Because My Grandson,
He's beautiful, beautiful in more ways than one
He takes your breath away
And your words come from the Heart

He's beautiful in more ways than one
He's the earth, the moon, the stars, the rising sun!
He's emerald, wheat, a precious pearl from the deep
A special gift sent from Heaven above
Addressed especially to everyone in this world to love

I felt so much beauty deep inside
The day he arrived on the Twelfth of May
The moment he opened his eyes
I knew where he came from
Because he's beautiful,
Beautiful, in more ways than one

He's beautiful, too beautiful for words to describe
All he has to do is look at me with those baby blue eyes
A warm liking sweeps over me

Elizabeth Browning would still be counting the ways
And Webster would still be adding words
'Cause My Grandson, he's beautiful,
Beautiful, in more ways than one!

Anthony Cardelli

My Grandson

My grandson
He's beautiful in more ways than one
As deep as a bed of pearls
As far as your eyes can see
That's how deep it runs
The beauty I feel in my grandson!

He's beautiful, beautiful in more ways than one
Heaven only knows how deep his beauty runs
For surely heaven is where he was sent from!

Rapped in a rainbow towel,
He came down floating on a snow white cloud
With a chorus of Guardian Angels singing on the wing
Under a galaxy of stars to chart the way
For him to arrive on the Twelfth of May!

He's beautiful, in more ways than one
The moment you look into his eyes,
You can feel where it all is coming from
It never stops, there is no end
It just runs and runs and runs!

He can make you laugh
He can make you cry with happiness
And the tears that fall feel so warm on your face
He can make you feel the warmth of the sun on a cold rainy day
With just a smile he takes your breath away!

A Man of Many Dreams

THE POWER OF BEAUTY

The power of beauty
Makes a blind man see
With the touch of his hand he feels inside where true beauty lies
He feels the warmth of the sun shining on his face
Rising within the coolness of the moon glowing, through the darkness of
the night
And the vibrations of the stars sparkling specs of light, spreading across
the sky

My grandson he's beautiful
Beautiful in more ways than one
With his moonbeam eyes that sparkle like diamonds in the sky
To chart the way through the cold darkness
Into the light of the rising sun
He's the moon! the stars! and the sun! all rapped into one!

My grandson he's beautiful
Beautiful in more ways than one
On the very first day he arrived,
I felt the beauty of happy tears swelling up in my eyes
Drowning the trail of sad tears behind

Sometimes the sun shines when it rains
It comes bursting through the clouds
Soaking up all the pain
With hand-painted rainbow towels!

Anthony Cardelli

Not for a Million

He's not worth two cents
But I wouldn't sell him for a million
What would I do with a million without him around,
To give me the things all the money in the world could never buy
I could never buy his kind of happiness with all that silver and gold
It could never buy the way he makes me feel way down deep inside
There are just some things money can't buy
Like the rising sun
He's beautiful in more ways than one

He's not worth two cents
But I wouldn't sell him for a million
Let alone all the treasures under the deep blue sea
I would be lost out there without the pleasure of the company of
My newborn Grandson!

He's not worth the time of day
But I wouldn't think of spending one day away from him
I would be lost without Anthony, my grandson!

A Man of Many Dreams

THE TWELFTH OF MAY

Wrapped in a rainbow towel
God sent him down
Floating on a snow white cloud
Under the star of Jupiter
Resting on the wings of a chorus of Guardian Angels
Guiding him down under a galaxy of crystal clear stars
Charting the way for him to arrive
On the Twelfth of May!

A. J.

A. J. is OK
Without him I feel blasé
When he shouts, "Papa"
It's the beginning of a bright new day

A. J. he's OK
My mornings are never blasé
I'm awaken by a comical, musical sound
Standing in his crib with both hands around the rim
Showing every rib he shouts out, "Papa"
Papa, you know it's the beginning of a bright new day
It's A. J.'s turn to live
And learn the facts of life and the fake of it

CHIP OFF THE OLD BLOCK

He's a chip off the old block
The spitten image of his "Pop"
He's solid stone, full of pearls from the depths
Breaching with emeralds into the sun
Seeding and sowing the sand into a land of wheat
To harvest each breath of life

Anthony Cardelli

"What's 'At"

I used to hate getting up every morning
Setting myself up for the daily routine
But would you believe getting up is a beautiful scene
For there standing in his crib is Anthony with a great smile!

Who would ever believe that now getting up is a beautiful scene
For as soon as I open my eyes, there's Anthony, smiling is his act
With an open question, "What's 'at"?

If I had my life to live over again, I would never let it end
Each day would be a new one for me
What has passed is past
Things are worthless if they don't last
I'm staging my life with a brand new cast
And ask, "What's' at"?

A Man of Many Dreams

I Couldn't Believe My Eyes

Listen to me, take it for what it's worth
Before you were born I was forty-eight
Now that's a lot of years, wouldn't you say?
For a guy to be ready to handle a little guy like you?
But you caught me by surprise
I couldn't believe my eyes when your father carried you in his arms
Wrapped in a rainbow towel
I saw the snow white cloud floating back to where you were sent from

Anthony, Anthony, Anthony—My Grandson
You're beautiful in more ways than one!

Pop

Anthony Cardelli

Raising a Boy

Although he'll break a brand-new toy
And everything else he gets his hands on,
There so much joy in raising a boy
Especially when God isn't finished with him yet

He repeats every word in the book
Page after page like a parrot in a cage
So you better be careful what you say
He may be on *Candid Camera* someday
He'll repeat everything you say
So be careful with your words
Because he's a sure bet to be a special guest
On *Candid Camera* someday

He's quick as a wink
Don't ever turn your back on him
Be sure to keep your eyes wide open
You can't afford the slightest blink
It will cost you your favorite set of dishes flying out of the sink
People will tell you he's just going through a stage

There's no telling what he'll do next
You can't foresee or foreshadow
This little lad goes on instinct like a parrot in a cage
He'll repeat everything you say
So be careful with your words
Because he's a sure bet to be a special guest
On *Candid Camera* someday

There's so much joy in raising a boy
That God hasn't finished yet
He breaks his toys when in a rage
But it does no good to scold him
He's going through a stage
He'll repeat every word like a parrot in a cage

A Man of Many Dreams

If you're not careful in what you say
You'll hear it from him the very next day

You can have fun with a son
And with a daughter your fathering days are never done
But when you have a grandson that's saying some
You know where he's coming from the moment he opens his eyes
And where he's going when he closed them for beddie-bye

He's a tough act to follow
With the quick changes of the many stages he's going through
He can make you laugh, he can make you cry
He can make you smile, He can make you frown
He can make you feel all these emotions at the same time
There's so much joy raising a baby boy

It's never dull when he's around
Like a parrot in a cage
A kid his age goes through so many stages
He's a tough act to follow
He picks you up on the very first note

Out of all the names I've been called throughout the years
From friends, foes, and fellow peers
Only one makes these old eyes cry happy tears that never stop
Is when Anthony calls me "Pop Pop"

Anthony Cardelli

Elizabeth Ann: June 16, 1978
My Pair of Queens

She's a Pair of Queens, Elizabeth Ann!
In the name of love she holds out her best hand
She's a whirlpool of pearls, emeralds, and wheat
The "class of the field" in any meet!

Though her heart skips a beat
She won't stop from doing the best she can
She's My Pair of Queens, Elizabeth Ann
Overflowing with love for her loved ones to feast!

She's a Pair of Queens, Elizabeth Ann!
Named after two beautiful ladies
She's too precious to hold
Too adorable to scold

Dressed in her christening gown
She's a Queen, hallowed with a triple crown
Glowing with love all around!

A Man of Many Dreams

EACH CHILD IS UNIQUE

Each child is unique
Look upon them and separate their time
Think back when you were their ages,
To set the stages of each mind

When you were two,
You could do what a one year old couldn't, of course
That's easy to see in Elizabeth and Anthony

Now as they grow older,
"Sissy Blue" will pick up the slack
And star in *My Fair Lady*
And Anthony, we were told by the utmost authority,
Will grow among the Red Woods and Holly
A "Sir Lancelot" of the forest
Galloping to Camelot

MY GRANDSON, MY GRANDDAUGHTER

Anthony & Elizabeth Ann
Try to do the best you can
And if that's not enough, give it another try
You have a lifetime to spend
Spend it well and you will dwell in the richness of life
Love and Happiness

I think the hardest of all things for people,
Is to fall in love with life
It would be wonderful if Anthony & Elizabeth Ann,
Would stay in love, as they are now, with Life

Anthony Cardelli

Emotions

He makes me laugh
He makes me burst into tears
He makes me happy to cry
He makes me mad,
To the point he makes me sad
And I dwell in between the well of his joy,
To make me glad
She makes me melt
She makes me pour all of me into
Her Heart!

The Charm of a Newborn

She makes me feel the warmth of the sun on a cold rainy day
The calm after the storm sailing around the Horn
The wonder and meaning of creation itself
The first time you enfold in your arms
The charm of a newborn!

More Beauty to Come

He's beautiful, in more ways than one
Heaven only knows how deep his beauty really runs
For Heaven is where he was sent from
Wrapped in a rainbow towel,
God sent him down floating on a snow white cloud,
Under the star of Jupiter to chart the way,
For him to arrive on the 12th of May!

Then came Elizabeth Ann
How much more beauty can one man stand!
And stand I did, tall as El Cid
I thought I saw it all in Anthony
But Elizabeth carried her own
Especially for me to see there's more beauty to come!

Anthony Cardelli

SHE ARRIVED: APRIL 29, 1980
DEANNA CATHERINE

She arrived sooner than expected
In fact her date was set weeks in advance,
Not to chance missing her going by
Now that she is here, I think it's time we all relax
And let nature take its course

She's too beautiful to have stayed away for so long
She's too beautiful for God to have waited any longer!

        I Love My Family!
Daddy

A Man of Many Dreams

DeAnna

"DeAnna"
I always liked that name
The first time its sound rung softy from a distance into my ears,
My eyes filled with Happy Tears
For the rest of my life to keep!

Up until now, "DeAnna",
Was just a name with a beautiful sound
But now, "DeAnna" is music to my ears
Forever in the background of
My Life!

Anthony Cardelli

GRANDCHILDREN

The beauty I missed when my eyes were too shallow to see,
Surrounds me now
I feel like a kid on a merry-go-round!
Catching the ring on the very first try
I feel like the same boy on a Christmas morning!
Playing with all the toys Old Saint Nick delivered the night before

NAMES

I've been called many names over the years,
By my friends, foes, and peers
Names with reason
Added with sounds sometimes not too pleasing to my ears
But somehow strange as it may seem,
Even though the names I've been called then,
Are still the same up until now
The last three people who have entered my life,
Drowned out the sound of all the names of my past
And way over the present

CARRY ON

All the beauty in Anthony, Elizabeth, and DeAnna
Is ours to enjoy for as long as we live
After we are gone, Joseph and Catherine will carry on
Until they pass away . . .
Anthony, Elizabeth, and DeAnna

Offsprings:
The Beauty They Carry

Anthony Cardelli

"Offsprings":
The Beauty They Carry

The rest of my days
How many I have left
Is anybody's guess, give or take a few, more or less

What ever the amount may be
It matters a great deal to me,
To spend them all with,
Elizabeth, DeAnna, and Anthony

Because they're beautiful,
Beautiful in more ways than one
Out of the spoils in my life,
God has cleansed My Soul
And poured into my shallow eyes,
The beauty of Elizabeth, DeAnna, and Anthony!

To feel how deep their beauty runs . . .
To the depths of the Precious Pearl
To the elegance of Emerald Green
And the strength of a Golden Harvest of Wheat

A Man of Many Dreams

A Note to My Grandson

I used to talk like you, walk like you
I even put on the same act like you
There isn't a single thing you're doing, that I didn't do
But then again, that's when I was young like you
Seeing you this way makes me feel all the beauty of my early yesterdays

When I was free as the wind!

Pop

Dear Anthony,

I'm like the kid who hollered fire and there was none
I made a joke once too often and it finally caught up to me
It's no fun going through life with the joke on thee
So if you want Pop Pop's advice, Anthony,
"Ice is to keep cool in summer . . . fire is to keep warm on winter nights"

Who Loves You?
Pop

Anthony Cardelli

BLOW YOUR OWN SMOKE

Summer is halfway through
Soon we will go into Fall
My family has been kept quite busy
Had no time for Summer play

All we have to do is look at Anthony
He's worth it all!
He's the third generation born in this country
I would like to be around and see what he does with it

If I see him sitting on his hands, I'll pass a grandfather's hint
Only amateurs sit on their hands and hope
Don't be a dope!
If you want to be a Pope, you have to blow your own smoke
Three white puffs is enough

A Man of Many Dreams

DOCTOR MARIN

He didn't ask me
He didn't tell me
He demanded
"Antonio, don't smoke"!
Don't drag yourself down
I know you want to see,
Your granddaughter's wedding gown
Standing tall on blessed ground

To stand tall on blessed ground
And see my granddaughters walk down the aisle
In their wedding gown!

Anthony Cardelli

For Elizabeth

For Elizabeth, the sun shows off his face
Shining right in her eyes the brightest smile
For Elizabeth, he opens the day in style
He follows her every step
Leading across the vast journey through life

For Elizabeth, for the beauty, one of the same
As the world turns on a new day, with or without the sun
She's beautiful in more ways than one
Someone once said not so long ago that beauty is a joy forever
Never before have truer words been spoken
For Elizabeth, joy endeavors

Elizabeth & Joseph Rocco's Wedding Day, June 27, 2009

ONCE AGAIN

Anthony, let me express what I felt on this day, May 12, 1977.

I was dancing on a cloud; proud as a peacock, standing tall in a crowd; bursting with joy. I just became a grandfather to a "baby boy"!
After forty-eight long years, you had me crying happy tears for making me see the future of Our Family Tree.

Now, on July 23, 2007, the happy tears are flowing for Gianna Marie. Words can't express the joy you and Jillian have given me only to say once again . . . I'm dancing on a cloud; proud as a peacock, standing tall for letting me see the future of the fourth generation of Our Family Tree!

Happy Birthday!
Love ya,
Pop-Pop

MY FAMILY

Once in My Life

I was right just once in My Life
And once is enough for me
Now that I look around,
And feel all the Love that surrounds me,
I'm looking forward to a beautiful future,
With the added branches of My Family Tree
God granted me life long enough,
To perceive the wonder and meaning of creation itself!

Annabella's Baptism March 9, 2014

Anthony Cardelli

NO PLACE LIKE HOME

I've been to many places but no matter where I roam,
In my heart I carry the place I call home
With its precious cargo I handle with care,
Treasured roots that continue to out grow
Within all the places I've been,
There's no place like home!
I found that out a long time ago

A Man of Many Dreams

LONG WAY FROM HOME

I'm a long way from home
But I'll never be afraid of the dark
'Cause there's always a candle burning in My Heart
From the flame in My Soul lighting the path to my way back home

You can have Paris in the Spring
London in the Fall
Rome all Summer long
I've been to them all
I know the feeling

But you'd be missing the whole thing,
If you don't feel the bite of Mr. Jack Frost nipping at your nose
Covering the three seasons with a sheet of ice under a blanket of white
Lighting up the stars to glow tiny crystals on the frozen lakes
Icy stilled streams with rainbows running in silence under the deep
The place to be on Christmas Eve
Home with family

Anthony Cardelli

THE ROOM THAT WARMED YOUR SOUL

She makes me feel as my eyes search into her,
The Summer in the Spring
The Winter in the Fall
The warmth of the sun on a cold rainy day
Blue charcoal burning in the kitchen
Pasta cooking in the pot on top of the lid
It sure felt good being in from the cold
In the one room that warmed your soul

MY HEART SKIPS A BEAT

My heart skips a beat
Every time I see your face
With your hair framing all of its beauty
Sitting in perfect posture

My heart skips a beat
Every time I see beauty
That's what beauty does to me
My eyes swell up in tears burning in the sun
With happy ones dropping one by one
I'm crying happy tears
Tears you never hold back
Tears you never hang up to dry
Tears that pour out of my eyes

A Man of Many Dreams

MY UNLOCKED HEART

I know what Love is all about
It's something I've never been without
It shows all over my face
Coming from a very special place,
Deep inside My Unlocked Heart

Since the day I was born,
I take it with me everywhere I go
I keep it in a very special place
Deep inside My Unlocked Heart

Anthony Cardelli

FEELINGS OF LOVE

Elizabeth Browning would still be counting the ways,
If she were alive today
To express how beautiful he makes me feel
From the time he arrived into this world

Sometimes the sun shines when it rains
Just when you think the end is near it suddenly appears
Bursting through the clouds
Soaking up all the pain with beautiful rainbow towels
Drying up all the tears that fell back inside
With its rays spreading over the skies
Changing the cold winds to tepid

Just when you think the game is going to be called on account of darkness

Love is charming, delightful, and gay
It makes you feel tender and warm throughout each day
It feels so cozy by a fireside roasting marshmallows
Melting frosted windowpanes
With the heat of love's passion rising

A Man of Many Dreams

LOVE

Love is good for whatever ails you
It can change an indigo mood into a swinging Basie tune
It can lift you when you're down on a crescendo of strings
Take you out of your silence breaking the sound barrier

PRICELESS

Love makes me feel charming delightful and warm
Soft and tender as a newborn

Love makes me feel the Summer in the Spring
The comfort from tepid winds,
Melting the Winter's frost

Love is priceless
It doesn't cost a thing
No matter were you shop
It's not for sale

LOVE GIVEN TO ME

I've had all kinds of love given to me
It never cost me a dime
From friends and relatives
And dear old mother of mine
Ever since the day I was born
When I came to love,
I was a winner every time!

Anthony Cardelli

MY EYES

My eyes will never stop searching,
The beauty I found in you
Because the deeper I go,
The more beautiful I feel
God only knows when it will end
But as long as He keeps it a secret,
I'll keep dwelling in its mystery

PLEASURE OF YOUR COMPANY

The pleasure of your company
Pleasures me the most
It still excites me so
Like a kid who can't wait to go out in the snow

It doesn't matter where we go
In the comfort of our home
Or out to a picture show
As long as you're by my side
The warm liking I feel,
Set by the flame in My Soul
Keeps the glow in my eyes

MY TIME WITH YOU

I hustle through the day
Doing what I have to do to earn my pay
Then when the clock strikes five, I become alive
Doing what I love best
To spend the rest of my time with you!

A Man of Many Dreams

WITHOUT LIMITS

Just to see you each day inspires me
Just to hear you talk is an inspiration
Just to smell the sweet fragrance you filter through the air,
Takes my breath away
Just to taste the flavor of Your Love,
Is more than I can say

And last but not the least,
Is the feeling of the sun rising in me,
From the warmth of Your Embrace

You're beautiful in more ways than one
Your beauty runs deep
It passes into and through me
Without limits, no boundaries

Anthony Cardelli

SHALLOW EYES

Shallow eyes
Only see the beauty My Love shows
They never feel where it's coming from
They see hair framing a face

Shallow eyes
Miss the beauty
She's beautiful in more ways then one

Shallow eyes
Never feel how deep it runs
They only see what's up front
Never will they know where her true beauty is coming from

What I thought I lost was right in front of my eyes
It was there all the time
But I was too blind to see through my swallow eyes
Fortunately for me, I'm one of the lucky ones who became aware,
He missed the beauty that was always there
And found myself deep into the joy of beauty forever!

A Man of Many Dreams

SINCE YOU CAME

Before you came into my life, my world was an empty shell
But now that you are here, my world is a carousel
Making beautiful sounds as it spins around
Mixing in the trade wind's musical lyrics,
For songbirds to sing to the many beautiful things that filled my world
Since you came into my life

THE BEGINNING OF A SYMPHONY

I never thought I could write a song
But since you came along strange things are happening to me
Words I never said before keep pouring out from deep within
And when I set them to the sound of my beating heart
It starts the beginning of a symphony

THE FRAMELESS PORTRAIT

I painted a Portrait of Life
And when I was through everyone who saw it,
Said it looked exactly like you

There was no doubt in their mind in what they saw,
On the face of the frameless portrait

She had your hair framing your tiny forehead
Your brows arched over your eyes shinning with Love

Anthony Cardelli

TO THE INFINITIVE

Just to see you walk inspires me
Just to hear you talk is an inspiration
Just to smell your trail of fresh scented fragrance,
Waters my lips for the sweet taste of the flavor in Your Love

Mixed with emotions not limited in person or number
You broke my fences, stepped over my defenses
And walked right in on all my senses
Every new sense we add a few branches,
To Our Family Tree

TRIPLE CROWN

You can tout me anytime
You never let me down
As far as I'm concern,
You're my "Triple Crown"
You're the class of the field
In the run for the roses
When it comes down to the wire,
The photo finish will show,
You nipped all their noses!

A Man of Many Dreams

WHEN YOU SMILE

When you smile
I see moonbeams dancing on the waves
I see stars falling out of place
To chart the way for the moon rays,
To light up your face shining in your eyes

When you smile
My world is a happy place to live in

When you laugh
My world is a carousel making beautiful sounds,
With the four season winds

When you're crying happy tears,
My world shines a full flower moon and sunshine rain

WE HAD IT ALL

Once we had it all
There was nothing left to be desired
Just the sound of your voice inspired me so
There wasn't a place on this earth we wanted to go
We had it all right here
Our own little world
We started with a shell
Filling it with Love in every room
Our special recipe from Our Hearts
We turned into a Home

Anthony Cardelli

UP UNTIL NOW

Up until now
I never saw the sun rising in the sky
It was always described through other eyes

Up until now
I never saw moonbeams dancing on the waves
I never saw the stars lighting up the sky
They, too, were always described through other eyes
That is, up until now

For now, I feel the warmth of the sun rising in me
I feel the vibrations of the ocean floor
I feel the stars glowing in your eyes
Charting the way, ending my search to Paradise

Up until now
I was just an eye witness to the beauty of God-Made Things
The sun, the moon and the stars, I took for granted
Would now forever shine on this beautiful planet

Up until now
"Love" was just a word among many in Webster's Dictionary
A no score in tennis and in certain other games
It's always left out in the rain
But as of now, a warm liking has swept over me
A fond and tender feeling touches My Sensitive Heart

A Man of Many Dreams

For now, I see for the first time in My Life
The beauty of all that was described right before my eyes
Through You, my feelings see through the blindness I was born with

Up until now
I felt my search had ended
All vibrations stopped leaving me drifting into space
That is, up until now
Because from the moment my eyes caught first sight of you,
I felt my search was just beginning
For as my eyes searched into your beauty I felt a new time and place
From just a glimpse of Your Beautiful Face!

Anthony Cardelli

WHERE MY HEART IS

The Summer evening breeze
Cooling off the long hot Summer's day
Willows bend, palms sway to the rhythm of our bodies
Swinging to and fro on a hammock between the trees
Breathing in the fresh scented fragrance from nature's seeds

People everywhere are searching for the best place to be
Lucky for me I found you
I don't have to search anymore
I found what I've been looking for

The best place for me is where you are
No matter where, as long as you are there
It's the best place for me by far

I've been to Paris, London, and Rome
But there's no place like home
And home is where you are
Wherever I go my body goes through the motions
And my mind wanders and it may roam
But home is where My Heart is!

MY GREAT GRANDCHILDREN

Gianna Marie Ciccia
Born July 23, 2007

Giuseppe Antonino Ciccia
Born February 11, 2010

Marco Joseph Rocco
Born September 4, 2012

Annabella Tessa Rocco
Born November 14, 2013

Marco Joseph & Annabella Tessa Rocco

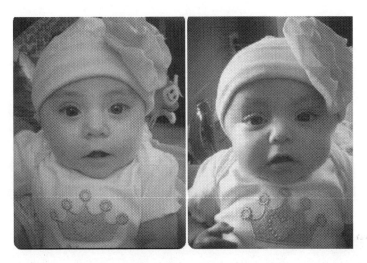

Twins Angelina Catherine Salzano & Giuliana Susan Salzano

Born May 14, 2014

DeAnna & Vince Salzano

SEASONS

A Man of Many Dreams

CHRISTMAS MOUNTAIN

Christmas Mountain
Her peaks tinged with snow
Evergreens dressed in red ribbon bows
Knotted through with a string of stars
That sparkle the crystals frozen in her branches through the pines
The icy stillness of the crystal lakes chills the air
Christmas Mountain

Rich with trees, wild plants, and streams
Living Saints dressed evergreen with red ribbon bows,
Dance in the rain clouds
And break the icy stillness of the lakes below

With rainbows rising to give us food, drink,
Physical power and understanding
Hills of thunder, resounding voices
Echo through the Heavens

Anthony Cardelli

AQUETONG ROAD

Aquetong Road
On the Pennsylvania side of the Delaware
At the very end of Washington Crossing Park
Take the first left, right on Aquetong Road
Trees high with fruit and leaves cross their branches
Blocking out the sun
But its rays find their way for you to follow through the thickest
To view the beautiful scenes of architect's dreams!

AUTUMN LEAVES

Autumn leaves golden brown amber and red
With a shade of left over Summer green
Cross their branches over Aquetong Road

I love when nature changes scenes
With just a brush of her hand
She paints over Summer green
A blanket of mixed colors in the Fall
Covering the ground with a blanket
To bed down under Winter's snow

AFTER THE TREES HAVE SHED

Paris in the spring
Rome in summer
London in the fall
Beautiful places to visit
After the trees have shed their leaves
To bed down on the ground for winters snow
It's the time best of the four seasons to be with family home on Christmas Eve

A Man of Many Dreams

A WELCOME SCENT IN THE AIR

There's a welcome scent in the air
Tepid winds fresh and clear
Spring is about to appear
Soon the flowers will bloom
The naked trees will be fully dressed
Vegetation will soon be ready to pick from the farms
While nature is changing her colors from winter's white
To spring and summer's green, red, and gold
People's faces will turn their frowns into smiles
And the sound of summer laughter
The long hot summer July through August
Before the leaves turn to shades of autumn

CRAZY, MIXED-UP DAY

The sun is shinning and it's raining
It's one of those crazy, mixed-up days
When Mother Nature can't quite make up her mind
So rather than let the day just pass by
She gave a little bit of both at the same time

For some people the sun shines every day
Even when skies are cloudy and gray
They can feel it's warmth on a cold rainy day

CrosbyBlue skies smiling over a White Christmas

Evergreens dressed in red ribbon bows
With a string of stars knotted through the pines,
To blink her eyes to light Old Rudy's nose,
To glow on Old Nicky dressed in red, tinged with snow
Cracking his whip by the light of the moon

Anthony Cardelli

CLOSE TO MOTHER NATURE

We had a stormy relationship that was wonderful
Was alive with excitement
Living with someone you can hate
And love at the same time
Close to nature when she can't make up her mind
Whether to let it rain or shine
So she gives us a little bit of both at the same time

The sun is shining and it's raining
Mother Nature is showing off today
Looks like she's going to show it all today
Clouds busting with bubbles mixing
Making beautiful colors
Bursting rainbows across the sky

FOUR SEASONS

Summer greens turning to Autumn's golden brown
Covered over with a blanket of Winter's white
I love the four seasons Mother Nature brings
She carries herself so well in the Spring

With just a wave of her hand
Tepid winds begin to thaw
The frozen tears upon the lips of Jack Frost
For him to taste the fresh bud sprouts of Spring

A Man of Many Dreams

GREAT TO BE ALIVE

There are over a million things in life
To make you feel great to be alive
Just to mention a few
Because the last thing I want to do is bore you

After a long hot Summer,
Doesn't it feel great to inhale a breath of fresh air,
From the leaves falling down
Laying a blanket gently on the ground
Isn't it great to cuddle in November
Lying in slumber by an open fire under a full moon
Nothing left to be desired

IT'S A MIRACLE

It's a miracle each morning rising with the sun
And see what Mother Nature has already done
While sleeping she was busy as a bee
Preparing a beautiful day just for me

Under the sun she painted a rainbow across the sky
And dabbed in a few white clouds rolling by
With a wave of her hand she brushed in tepid winds
With the sound of a crescendo of strings
To begin a symphony of birds
Singing on the wings of Spring

Anthony Cardelli

MOTHER NATURE

Sometimes Mother Nature goes out of her way
And pours out everything she has into one day
She begins with a brush of her hand
And paints the sun rising over the land
And from the peaks tinged with snow,
She dabs the sky with white clouds bursting with rain
To drop into the tepid winds
To spray rainbows from end to end

MOTHER'S DAY

With happy tears, with sadden tears
She sheds from her eyes
Streams of love and pain flowing down her face
Falling through space on the fresh buds of Spring

With each tear she drops, her flavors mix
The scented fragrance of nature
To sprout in full bloom in the month of May
Blessed gifts of life for Mother's Day"

A Man of Many Dreams

SPRING

When God made the world
He filled it with everything
I like to think He began with a crescendo of strings
To lift the birds on the wing to carry in the tepid winds
To thaw the winter's frost with warm healing waters
To fall on the sleeping birds under a blanket of snow
And open their eyes to the colors of Spring

ONE SPRING MORNING

One Spring morning
I awakened to the sound of a beautiful melody I never heard before
And as I listened in silence these lyrics came to mind
From the sound that opened my eyes

The beauty of first light from the brush of nature's hand
Painting under open skies the sun rising over the land
Brushing in tepid winds swaying the willows
Bending to the beckon call of the first buds of Spring
Sprouting from the thaw the warm April showers bring

From the brush of nature's hand she paints with natural colors
On her canvas under open skies
Brushing away the darkness, the beauty of first light

With the sun rising over the land brushing in tepid winds
Spraying with April showers
To sway the willows to bend to the beckon call
Of the first buds of Spring spouting from the thaw

Anthony Cardelli

LULLABY OF SPRING

I wake up each morning
To the sound of nature's alarm
Before I open my eyes
I feel the warmth of My Love
Wrapped in my arms

And as the world turns on a new day
A crescendo of strings lifts the sun over a new horizon
As my concerto begins
My eyes open to the sound of the Blue Jay
Singing the lullaby of Spring

YOU'RE THE REASON

I love you in Winter, when snow begins to fall
I love you in the Spring, when ice begins to thaw
I love you in the Summer, when it's time to play ball
I love you in the Autumn, when leaves begin to fall
You're the reason I love not one, but the whole four seasons

SPELLBOUND

As the moon suddenly appears
As the sun slowly descends
Twilight colors spread throughout the sky
Your eyes are wide open shut
As you are spellbound at the sight
And as soon as it fades away to end a twelve hour day
The moon and the stars light up the night
To begin the colors created by the moon's light
To chart the way from Barnegat Bay to Ole Cape May

January 31, 2012

GOD'S LOVE

Anthony Cardelli

A STORY CENTURIES OLD

A story centuries old is still being told
A story passed on from man to man
Over sea and land
To guide lost souls who went astray
Traveling on Trilogy Road

With only a star to chart their way,
Three wise men left their caravans with riches and spices
And galloped over the waves of the singing sands
On ships of the desert

Three total strangers meeting in a manger
To bare witness of a new born baby
Eternal Life
Delivered in God's Hands

A Man of Many Dreams

BEFORE MAN

Before Man
God laid down the seeds
And covered the ground with earth
With a wave of His hand He sowed in the wind
To carry the rain falling on His Garden of Eden

With His eyes He lifted the sun over the clouds
Bursting with rainbows arching across the skies
Before Man,
This land was Paradise!

FROM SEEDS TO A RAINBOW

When all eyes end their search
And feel through the darkness into the light,
Then every human being will feel warm as me
No hands will be cold
Warmed over the eternal flame of all souls
Burning the silver and gold
To melt down in the heart, the purity of precious pearls
With the elegance of emeralds
Growing the body with the strength of golden wheat
That's when the seeds God planted from the beginning,
Will sow for all souls to reap
A rainbow from end to end!

Anthony Cardelli

God-Made Things

From the peaks tinged with snow
Down to the palms where balmy breezes blow
Trading with the winds of the seven seas
All the splendor of God-Made Things

Summer tides raising the ocean's floor
With moon beams dancing on the waves
With the galaxy lighting up the stars,
To chart the way of the sea castles sailing through the fog

To catch the glow of ice candles,
Floating on course of the captain's log
God-Made Things are all around us

God's Gift to Me

As my eyes search your beauty,
I perceive the wonder and meaning of creation itself
I feel joy everlasting
I feel happiness in all its sadness
For you are God's gift to me, sent from the heavens above
Addressed especially for me to love
Fulfilling my soul to keep its flame glowing over my heart,
To pour out to you
Lighting my way through the darkness

A Man of Many Dreams

GOD'S KIND OF LOVE

When you give all you have to receive just a smile
When you put food into the mouth of a starving child
You're giving God's Kind of Love

When you give a cup of water to those who thirst
When you bind the wounds of those who hurt
Among the many Hawks, to turn just one into a Dove
That's God's Kind of Love

What kind of love is it that makes a Hawk turn into a Dove?
What kind of love is it that gives a cup of water to those who thirst?
God's Kind of Love

What kind of love is it that makes a blind man see?
What kind of love is it that binds the wounds of those who hurt?
God's Kind of Love

What fools we mortals be
Never to feel God's Kind of Love
The ones that do, are in the minority

To turn the other cheek
Facing humility strengthens the meek
To turn a Hawk into a Dove
That's God's Kind of Love
To give up all the treasures hoarded in life,
In exchange for one cup of rice,
To put into the mouth of a starving child,
To feel the joy of just a smile
To melt all the silver and gold and turn it into wheat and rice
That's God's Kind of Love

Anthony Cardelli

What fools we mortals be
That only see the pond
For our eyes are too shallow to feel how deep it runs

To turn the other cheek
To show the strong the strength in the meek
Turning the Hawk into a Dove
That's God's Kind of Love

To guide a Lost Soul to the heavens above
That's God's Kind of Love
What fools we mortals be
Not to believe in what we see!

A Man of Many Dreams

OLD FATHER TIME

Old Father Time and me
We go back along way
He was more than a father to me
With his eyes he watched over me,
As I searched with mine
And with his grace of time,
He made me feel inside the beauty
The shallow surface

ON A MIDSUMMER'S NIGHT

On a Midsummer's night
The Summer tide came crashing upon the shore,
Raising the ocean's floor
As moonbeams were dancing on the waves
As my eyes searched through the clouds,
I felt beyond my time and place
For there up in the sky was a fleet of sea castles on the horizon

THE PROMISED LAND

The sun shines to heat up the day
The moon glows to cool off the night
The stars sparkle to chart the way for me to follow
The footsteps you left behind in the sand
To the Promised Land

Anthony Cardelli

PRAYER

Lord give me another chance
There's a lot of good left in me
Give me the chance to try once more
To restore the good I gave
And took away the happiness,
I brought to someone special
Don't let me leave the sadness

ONLY ONCE IN A LIFETIME

Only once in a lifetime
Will be enough to live through eternity
To rise and bare witness to the Resurrection

Only once in a lifetime
Is all it takes to feel God's Love
When you first embrace its fullness swelling up in your face
With Your Soul burning a blue flame glowing in your eyes
Showing the fulfillment of all His Grace
Deep inside Your Heart

A Man of Many Dreams

PARTNERS OF NATURE

God created the earth for all things to inhabit
His spiritual voice resounded from the Heavens above
Off the peaks tinged with snow
Wind to be carrying the Word through the clouds below
Over the hills and dales

God created the earth for all things to inhabit, not just man
When man perceives the wonder and meaning of creation itself,
His thoughts will not perish
They will enrich the soil where he returns to the ground

With trees rich with fruit and leaves, wild plants and streams
Streams running with silver and gold pouring from the lakes
Filled with rainbows rising, glittering in the sun for man to spare
And give food, drink, physical power, and understanding
To offspring sprung and to sprout into full bloom,
Partners of nature again

STANDING ON THE MOUND

Standing on the mound
Overlooking the baked tablelands below
As my eyes search through the clouds high above peaks, tinged with snow,
Resounding voices a million light years away,
Answered the prayers of my fathers before and after me
For I felt beyond my time and place, as I stood there on the mound
Searching deeper into the last frontier

Living Saints dressed evergreen danced on the rain clouds
Descending healing waters, to break the icy stillness of the blue lake,
To run down the brooks and streams
Pouring silver and golden rainbows into the hands of the "Fisherman"
To share in food and drink
Understanding the wonder and meaning of
God-Made Things

Anthony Cardelli

THE CRACK OF DAWN

Up before the crack of dawn
To inhale the ray of first light
And let out a sigh of relief
From a good night's sleep
As my eyes search
A warm liking feeling swept over me
I felt the sun rising through me

THE EYES OF THE WORLD

The eyes of the world must be too shallow to see what's going on
For shallow eyes never feel the beauty deep inside God-made things
The eyes of the world stopped searching for His label
For God-made things, don't have any
Even shallow eyes, such as mine, recognize God-made things
They never lose their shine

THIS SIDE OF HEAVEN

There's a special place on this side of Heaven
Full of God-Made Things
High above the clouds, peaks tinged with snow,
Melt down to the palms where balmy breezes blow
Trading with the winds of the seven seas
All the splendor of God-Made Things

Grassy hillocks surrounded with trees shading out the sun
But some of its rays find their way
Through the riches of the fruits and leaves
The creation of architect's dreams

A Man of Many Dreams

SOMEWHERE THIS SIDE OF HEAVEN

Somewhere this side of heaven
There's a special place called "God's Country"
Although it has no sign it's so easy to find
I can tell you how to get there and it won't cost you a dime
Just follow the sun until day is done
Then turn any which way into twilight
You can catch any moonbeam glowing on the stars
To chart your way to Paradise!

THE GIFT

From the moment I open my eyes,
My feelings deep inside pour out to life,
The blessed gift, given to me each day
To spend as I wish with heavenly bliss
To kiss the buds that sprout in May
Each moment of life no matter how spent,
Is the gift we have on our lease in life

ONLY GOD

The world survived another threat
The know it alls were paying out bets,
To the people who believed,
The world would never end

Only God will tell you when,
The world will come to an end
The day that happens, as quick as a wink,
The world will disappear

January 31, 2012

LIFE

A Man of Many Dreams

LIFE

I can't write no more
It doesn't make any sense
All the words in the puzzle of life have yet to solve its mystery

I'm afraid it's impossible for me to fit them all
If we can find the right words to fit the puzzle called Life,
Then the whole world would know what it's all about

If we all at one time set our watches and search with our eyes,
Then the whole world will feel its mystery
All questions and answers will be obsolete
When the last word completes the puzzle called Life

TRILOGY ROAD

Trilogy Road
No one knows how far it goes
There's no way to measure between then, now, and when,
On a road that never ends
There are no signs to guide you on Trilogy Road
No one ever found it on the map

On Trilogy Road no one knows how far they will travel
I think it takes a lifetime but your guess is as good as mine
A road with no signs, with or without eyes, you travel on Trilogy Road
Through then, now, and when

THEN, NOW, AND WHEN

The world is a carousel
Spinning with lyrics and music clear as a bell
She rings through the night to light up the sky
As the moonbeams on the stars to chart the way,
Of the many souls traveling on Trilogy Road

Anthony Cardelli

The only road to leave a past
As you keep going with the present pace
Never wanting to stay in one place

Until you reach the future on Trilogy Road
There are only three signs to follow
Then, now, and when
As your passing by them you can look back
And see up until now
But our eyes are too shallow to feel the sign
To when Trilogy Road ends

It Takes a Lifetime

It takes a lifetime,
To travel to the end of Trilogy Road
A road not like all roads that lead to Rome
They have all been measured and mapped
Trilogy Road can't be measured by a ruler or tape
Time is the distance from then, now and when

It takes a lifetime,
To pass through the many happy stations of days gone by
And strange as it may seem an eternity, when you overtrained
In between the raindrops, off the track,
To a nearby sad station along the way

A Man of Many Dreams

A HOBO ON THE RAILS

My way of passing by, passing through
Making my way, each day is passing me by
I'm catching stages, hopping rides
A Hobo on the rails
Laying down the track to new trails

A Hobo on the rails
We'll name him John Doe
A man on the streets of the world
Walking with life until death do part

Ms. Joan Doe walks with life
And when the twain meets the world will spin around
And around and around
Like when you were a kid on a Merry-Go-Round
Watching the whole world spinning around
Valentines tinged with expressions in the snow

A PLACE WITH NO NAME

I heard of a place where the sun shines every day
And it only rains to wash bitter memories away
Then the clouds roll by to dry your eyes with beautiful rainbow towels
This place has no name but it's easy to find
All you have to do is leave the past behind
Your wounds will heal with the grace of time
And all the bitter memories will burn out of sight, out of mind

Anthony Cardelli

ALL I EVER WANTED

All I ever wanted were the simple things in life
Nothing complicated, things that are easy to handle
Things that would never break even under the hottest pressure
And all I would have to give back is the precious gift it gave me,
Tender loving care

For all I ever wanted was the pleasure of your company
Cause every time we would get together,
You know what use to please me the most?
The pleasure of your company

All I ever wanted were the simple things in life
Things that wouldn't break under the slightest pressures
Easy to handle with tender loving care

A Man of Many Dreams

ALL ROADS LEAD TO ROME

All roads lead to Rome
No matter where you start
Each road was measured and mapped
For you to follow with your heart

All roads lead to Rome
The city that lights up the flame of each soul
To burn eternally with love

BUSINESS FOR SALE

I'm selling away a part of my life
Which has nothing to do with the price
What you're paying for is standard equipment
Just like new if you have the polish
The sun will keep shinning through on your smiling face
Glowing with the true investment you made

LIGHT ON THE BET

I tried to get to where I wanted to go too fast
I skipped a few steps in the past
Causing me to trip and fall
I didn't get anywhere at all
So here I am heavy in debt
Light on the bet

Anthony Cardelli

THROWING IN THE TOWEL

There were times in my life
When I felt like throwing in the towel
Giving up on all my hopes and dreams
Tired of coping with the same routine

MAN

Superior to none
When it comes to getting the job done
He never starts anything he can't finish
He never fell behind the lead

Since his time began
From one million BC to nineteen eighty
Lady Luck is still his favorite charm
And when his time comes to be counted
He'll proudly stand
For he is Man

TWO CANDLES

She said a prayer for all who passed away
She said a prayer for all who are living today
Two candles she burns in front of your Grace
On her knees she kneels bowing her head
With her hands cupping her face

A Man of Many Dreams

FOR SOME PEOPLE

For some people the sun shines every day
It seems to follow them every which way
Even when it rains they find a way to walk in between
And come through without a drop falling through the clouds
Wrapped in a rainbow towel from head to toe

BENDING IN THE WIND

How many times in my mind I keep changing it,
I lost count of, only you understand what I just said
So, I'll tell you the whole story
Because I know you'll want to hear the end
So, I'll start in the middle, then to the beginning
And save the best part for the end

In the middle, I was in between My Heart and mind,
Mixed up all the time
In the beginning with my wings clipped I soared into the glory of life!
And now in the end my wings are bending in the wind

Anthony Cardelli

DON'T HOLD BACK THE TEARS

To Whom It May Concern

This is for people who loved in vain
People who put up all they had
Only to be left with the feeling of everlasting pain

Don't hold back the tears
Let them fall out of your eyes
If you hold back the tears
They will keep dropping back inside
On all the pain down deep
In a place where the sun never shines after it rains

Don't hold back the tears
Let them fall out of your eyes
Don't hold back the tears
That has been drowning all your dreams inside

A Man of Many Dreams

FROM THE OLD SCHOOL

I'm from the old school
I play for keeps
A one-nighter I was never cut out to be

But the kids today,
Don't see it that way
Although the school they attended,
Is still in the same place

I TOLD YOU SO

When you're the last to know
The last thing you want to hear is,
I told you so
It hurts too much to show the pain you feel,
Seeing a face grinning from ear to ear

THE OTHER GUY

Gee, I've got it rough
But not as tough as the other guy
The one who walks beside me
I knew it wouldn't be easy
But it's not as hard as the other guy behind me

Anthony Cardelli

How Do You Know?

A question most ask of me is . . .
How do you know when love is real?
My only answer is that I can't answer with just one word
Take for instance . . .
Elizabeth Browning just kept on counting the ways to express how it
feels
And Webster defined right down to the bottom line,
Under the letter L what to feel
And last but not least, it was set to music to add confusion,
To an already confused society
With the likes of Porter, Cahn, and Van Heusen

How

How much of the world does one person need to live in?
How much of the world does one person want if he can't have it all?
It shouldn't matter how small or tall a person is
We all come from the same place
And the world has plenty of space for all of us to fit

A Man of Many Dreams

In Better Times

In better times better thoughts ran through my mind
Apples blossomed, flowers bloomed
Skiing over the peaks tinged with snow
Sailing a lake with rainbows rising over the quake we made in the waves
Glittering of silver and gold arched in front of the horizon we passed

In better times better thoughts ran through my mind
All bridges were easy to cross
You never had to wait in line
There was enough room for everyone walking to the other side

Until one day the Bomb Bay doors opened
And the bombardier who operates the bombsight
Released the mechanism on the first note of "Bombs Away"
Dropping on target on the many bridges that were once easy to cross
The gap in between life and death is how wide you span
How far into life's vast journey will you travel before your span runs out,
To rise or fall?

Anthony Cardelli

IN THE PRIME OF MY LIFE

In the prime of my life,
I had the time of my life
The world was my oyster and I dwelled in its shell,
Lying on a bed of pearls
Turning every stone into shinning emeralds,
From the strength of the golden wheat I seeded and sowed

Yes, in the prime of my life
I would rise with the sun and follow it through the day
Transcending into twilight
Feeling the warmth in the smile of the moon, glowing over the stars,
To chart my way through the darkness of the night

In the prime of my life,
I faced the high winds and weathered the storm
Breezed through the calm
And at the same time with awareness of nature's quick changes

A Man of Many Dreams

IS THERE SUCH A PLACE

Is there such a place
Where people celebrate Christmas every day?
When a story centuries old is forever being told
Not just once a year

A place where nothing is left out
The more the merrier is welcomed in
To a fresh start from the Original Sin
To carry the Gift of Life, heavy or light

Following the star called Jupiter to chart their way,
Through the darkness of the night
Over the waves of the singing sands
Melting down to cool from baking in the desert sun

KICK OUT OF LIFE

To teach old dog new tricks, is a kick in life
To be able to get through the shield without getting burned,
Now that's a kick out of life!

To distinguish the same would be absolutely insane
For never the twain shall meet
Like that little doggie in the window,
That never got to go with "Alice Blue Bonnet"
And "Johnny Fidora"
Now that's a kick somewhere else in life!

Anthony Cardelli

TWO FOR THE PRICE OF ONE

Throughout your life you get
Two for the price of one
There will be days when half is better than none
Who really gets what they want out of life?
I haven't heard from them yet
I only listen to those who settle for what they need

LAST CALL

Until last call that's how long I'll stay
That's when I know it's time to go
I keep time with a barmaid
Who doesn't have to look at the clock
To know when to say, "Last call for alcohol"

She keeps her ears and eyes open
To the sound of the crowd
And when they start getting nasty and loud
And their laughing clown faces turn into frowns
Before they start spinning the barrel around like a ball
She screams from the top of her lungs
To quiet down them all
"Last call for alcohol"

A Man of Many Dreams

MERRILY WE ROLL ALONG

We both know we can't have the life we really want for each other
But we can make the best of it each time we see another
We now have the kind of certainty which is very rare in couples of the past
But in our present state of mind we are going to get along just find

Training my thoughts on a track in reverse
Passing by happy stations when everything came naturally
Nothing rehearsed; there were no false parts
Two people knowing their lines came from the heart

Yes, we had our angry moments, of course, but just a few
Only moments, no more, because we knew we had this good thing going
There I go again, couldn't resist adding a few lines from Stephen Sondheim
From the musical "Merrily We Roll Along"
I never seen the play, but I went to Carnegie Hall
When Frank Sinatra was appearing there in the month of September
He sang the song reading from the music sheet
He wasn't sure of the lyrics
Another lesson added to the price of admission

Anthony Cardelli

NIGHTCAP

I've seen it happen often enough
One is too many and too many is not enough
I've seen it happen time and time again
Just one more for the road leading to nowhere

The nightcap that keeps popping in the air
I've felt loneliness and despair
Behind the mask they wear
Painted smiles with stylish laughter

MILLIONS ON THE RUN

Millions on the run
On the dark side of the sun
Creeping like snails underground
Following a trail of tears
Filled with broken dreams of the yesteryears
Of mixed emotions and illusions of confused societies

Millions on the run
Running in silence
The power of survival on a non stop flight
Through the darkness of the night
In search of a place to hide
From the light of the day breaking away
From the dark side of the sun

A Man of Many Dreams

TREES

Trees grow the old-fashioned way
From the bottom they start
And they don't stop until they get to the very top
Wouldn't it be a fine thing if all human beings
Would follow the ways of the trees?

Trees stand tall no matter how big, how small
They know when to bend to knee-level winds
They're wise to the storm and face it through the calm
Wouldn't it be a fine thing if all human beings
Would follow the ways of the trees?

SPINNING

The world keeps spinning on a plate
Dishing out love and hate
As the centuries roll by,
We are left with more hate
More hate than we can take
Tilting the plate
To break into an earthquake
I'm spinning on a disc
Gold and silver-plated
Stepping on the stars

TIME: THE TATTLETAIL OF LIFE

Each tick of the clock
Clips another lock of hair
Time turns it gray
When it stays on too long
Hair mixed in time
To begin the first tick of the clock
To clip a lock

Anthony Cardelli

ONLY TIME WILL TELL

Only time will tell
When you make your dream come true
Time will tell on you

Only time will tell
When you strike it rich
Melting down pure gold with the flame of your soul
Pouring into your wishing well
Time will tell on you

Only time will tell
It's been around for quite a while
It tells Mother Nature what course to take
Didn't you ever stop to wonder why there's always a smile on her face?

POOR LITTLE RICH GIRL

Poor little rich girl
Her wealth buys everything she wants
But the one thing she needs
Surrounded by people inherited along with all her treasures
Is left without the pleasures of the company she keeps

Poor little rich girl
Never will she find the Love she seeks
Living a life of fun and games
Out in the open under the sun
Behind closed doors when it rains
 Poor little rich girl
Never will she gain playing games
Where all the rules are the same
In or out of doors where love is a no score

Poor little rich girl
Longing to inhale Love in the air she breathes

A Man of Many Dreams

SAD AND HAPPY PEOPLE

Sad people always have a story to tell
Happy people know so well
They listen never to be bored
For they were there before

Happy people never have to tell a story
With their eyes searching in the distance
They can easily see beyond their time and place
They perceived the wonder and meaning of Creation itself

Happy people feel the Summer in the Spring
Feel the colors changing in the Fall, as the trees undress
Dropping their leaves to cover the ground
Spreading a blanket of nature's paintings all around

Happy people never have a story to tell
Sad people know ever so well
From the smile on their faces
Compared to the frown on theirs
The look of sadness would be out of place
So, sad people tell their story to themselves
Going through life, telling the same old story of living in Hell

Anthony Cardelli

WHERE WERE YOU?

Where were you
When your baby cried in the middle of the night?
Were you there to wipe the tears of fear from her eyes?
Pray, tell me, where were you?

Where were you
When she took her first step?
Were you there to break her fall?

Where were you
When she learned to use the phone?
Were you there to answer her call?

Where were you
When she smeared on Mommy's lipstick and rouge?
Wearing her oversized clothes and awkwardly walking
In her high-heel shoes
Were you there to capture the rapture of her youth?
Pray, tell me the truth, where were you?

Where were you
When she needed you the most?
When her first love turned out to be just a hoax
Were you there to explain puppy love isn't the same?
Until the real thing comes along

A Man of Many Dreams

THE BITTER TASTE

She's willing to accept,
What her mother and father have done
Trying to understand that half,
Is better than none

When she was born,
Up until the time her mother and father made the break,
She had the whole cake

She's grown up enough to know,
That it will take more than a bottle of Scope,
To take away the bitter taste

TOUGH LOVE

Tough love
Is so easy to come by
It's a far cry from the soft touch of a love under a full flower moon

She knows how it feels to meet tough love head on
She got herself knocked head over heels and laid flat on her back
Taking the count of ten before the crack of the bell
She knows all too well never to fall into its spell

Anthony Cardelli

The Courage of Billie Jean

She didn't let the love she was dealt with slip through her fingers
She held on tightly to the King of Hearts in her hand
Tall as a redwood, he backed up her stand to support the willow in her life
Bending to knee level winds that suddenly came blowing in

Billie Jean, bent with the willow, as she did on the opposite side of the net
In the game of tennis, love can tangle you up in its web
And miss love's call, which means nothing at all to the points on the board
Because love is a no score in tennis and in certain other games

The courage of Billie Jean was as strong as her King of Hearts
She didn't let the love she was dealt in her hands slip through her fingers!

The Eyes and Ears of the World

In the middle of the forest
I can hear a tree falling silently

In the middle of a crowd
I can hear someone falling just as loud
With all the pain in the world
It's a wonder why no one feels the teardrops falling back inside

The answer must be
The eyes and ears of the world are shallow and hollow
And their stomach is too weak to swallow

A Man of Many Dreams

THOROUGHBREDS

I never play the favorites
I like to pick my own losers
But all kidding aside,
It's a thrill to see an apprentice boy on a maiden
Riding by Fillies and Geldings
And cross the finish line by a nose ahead of the mare

Thoroughbreds they do it all
Pure, nice, and neat
They're all so thoroughly trained
Never to overstrain the track
A well-bred breed
That just loves when the wheat turns to hay
Am I talking about horses?
Am I talking about people?

Anthony Cardelli

WHAT FRIENDS ARE FOR

You can always count on them
When you need someone to talk to
Someone to relate to, it's for sure
That's what friends are for

You can always count on them
When you need someone to talk to
When the one you were close to isn't there anymore
That's what friends are for

You can pour out all your feelings
When they become too heavy to carry
They pick up each emotion
That's what friends are for

You can always count on them
When you need someone to talk to
Someone you don't have to answer to
That's what friends are for

They know when it rains it pours
They saw the tears that never fell,
On the game they knew had ended a long time ago
But they would never say, "I told you so"
That's what friends are for

A Man of Many Dreams

The Second Chance on the First Impression

The beauty you missed is still out there
Waiting to be enjoyed
The second chance on the first Impression you made
Is waiting to be taken

Nothing is lost that can't be found
Life's changing scenes in between acts
Cause you to play the many parts of a clown
With painted faces of sadness and tears
Smeared with grease that leaves a stain over the years

Women in My Life

The women in my life, where shall I begin
The beginning is as good a place as any
My life began inside my mother
Until the time came for her to labor my life,
Into the midwife's hand
To slap my first outcry into life

With the slap of the midwife's hand
The first outcry to life begins
From then up until now,
The world has been a great big merry-go-round
Making beautiful sounds on every turn
Spinning the lyrics to mix into the beautiful melodies
Of each song, sung

Anthony Cardelli

WHEN YOU ARE YOUNG

When you are young
You carry the past so well
For the world is your oyster
And you dwell in its shell
Picking up the pearls not too deep
Just the ones that lie at your feet

AS YOU GROW OLDER

There's nothing wrong with having fun
That's the most important part of keeping yourself young
As long as you're aware of the things to come as you grow older
There's nothing right about mistakes
That's part of life
As long as you're aware of the wrong as you grow wiser
You may call me stupid now
But as you grow older, you'll realize how wise a stupid person can be

A Man of Many Dreams

THE ESSENCE OF LIFE

To receive the pleasures in life from you,
Would be a dream come true
For you to want the pleasures in life from me,
Would be too true to dream
To recapture the rapture in the reality I once knew,
Is my life's goal!

To rekindle the flame of My Soul
To spark the coals of My Heart
To warm these hands that were too cold
To touch the glow from the moon I see on your face
To feel the warmth of the sun from your embrace
To hear with reason a sound well seasoned
With flavors of your love to taste
And the pleasing smell of a sweet fragrance scented from your grace

To recapture my five senses
To break down all the fences
To build strong defenses
To withstand the strongest offenses
Is the Essence of Life!

Anthony Cardelli

ONLY HEAVEN KNOWS

A story centuries old is still being told
To guide the many Lost Souls,
Traveling on Trilogy Road
A road not measured in width and length
But a road measured in time spent
Its distance is from then, now, and when

Each one of us can measure from then and now
From the day we're born to the age of no return
But only Heaven knows when our time will end

ANOTHER LOST SOUL

I missed the beginning and now I'm trying to catch up in between
To perceive before it ends what life really means
No one knows the true distance from then, now, and when
But I'll keep traveling on Trilogy Road searching for a sign
Before time takes its toll from another lost soul

A Man of Many Dreams

The Secret of Living

Think young and you'll never grow old
For age is only a number of time to pay the toll
Your cost of living, is your life
It's yours to spend on happiness and love
On your way to the heavens above

The secret of living is to fall in love with life
Like taking in deep breaths of fresh scented roses,
The April showers bring
For it's great to be alive in the Spring
Love life and all living things around you
Be true to yourself
No matter how false people can be

Recipe for Happiness

To love and be loved in return
Have enough money left over to burn
Set yourself in the right direction
Getting a little more out of life than expected

Mix these four ingredients and pour it into your nest
And stir until it's at its best
That's my recipe for happiness

Life's End

Where will the trail lead to from the last step I leave behind?
Is still the question unanswered in my mind
The mystery of life's end is still unsolved as it revolves on its axis
With time never stopping as we drop and fall out
One by one off the line of life

SELF-REFLECTING

A Man of Many Dreams

ALL MY YESTERDAYS

All my yesterdays are backing up on me
I have no place to put today except in front of me
Blocking my way to a better tomorrow

For all my yesterdays are cascading in from behind
Drowning all my dreams,
That will never stand against the knee-level winds
Shaking the ground under me

All my yesterdays are in my way for a better tomorrow
I have no place to put today after it's through
There's no room left behind me
With all my yesterdays running over me,
There's no space left for me to borrow

All my yesterdays were well worth living through
For what I feel today makes them all just as new,
Is because of you!

Anthony Cardelli

Without an Education

Without an education
I traveled to faraway places in my imagination
Leaving my body behind

All those in favor of giving Love a chance
Raise your hands up high
And cup your palms for all the doves to soar from above
And pour a portion of their Love to all of us
To spill over the land!

Among the Many Millions

Among the many millions
I always count myself as one
Each morning I rise with a new pair of eyes and follow the sun
And as my eyes search into the twilight
I latch on a moonbeam shining brightly on the star
To chart my way through the darkness of the night

Among the many millions
I count myself as one
Running on the dark side of the sun
Running in silence
The power of survival that keeps the dream alive
For all those behind me

A Man of Many Dreams

As Long as a Lifetime

I get back to myself whenever the opportunity arrives
I put myself in drive and ride on a one-way street to the end of the line
It wouldn't really be me to turn back in time
To live in a dream that's over and done with
Reality is now; it's what and who you are in the present
Not who and what you were then
How long we travel on Trilogy Road only heaven knows when
But your guess is as good as mine
I figure it takes as long as a lifetime

At This Stage of the Game

At this stage of the game
You would think by now
All that we lost would be covered by what we gained
But the fact is not in our imagination
But in the reality that still remains

In the beginning we know it wouldn't be easy
But at this stage of the game
We never dreamed it would be this hard
Thinking back, there were times when the load became too heavy to carry
But together we weathered through knee-level winds

Anthony Cardelli

BETWEEN THE RAINDROPS

I've been walking in between the raindrops
Singing in between the notes of past melodies
It's time to get my feet wet
And step into what's really going on
With a new pair of eyes and a new pair of shoes
Feeling in my bones when it's gonna rain or shine

I've been walking on a melodic time
Never feeling the sun shinning on my face
Never tasting the raindrops falling on my lips
Never hearing the sound

IT MIGHT HAVE BEEN

Words of wise men left behind for future thoughts,
Scribbled through my mind
Among the many these words kept falling back in line,
On the track of the train of my thoughts

The saddest words from tongue and pen
The saddest are these, "It might have been"

Only I can see all the undeveloped negatives,
That are still hanging up to dry
In the darkroom of my mind

A Man of Many Dreams

NOT THE GARBO TYPE

I don't want to be alone
I'm not the "Garbo type"
I like to mingle and mix
Searching in the crowd
Digging deep into their shallow eyes
Certain to find one who feels the same as I
I like to smoke my pipe and pass it on
Speak my piece to release some steam
Then go to bed with my favorite dream

ENOUGH TO GET BY

My youth flew the coop
I didn't give it the chance to nest
I left ahead of my time
I was in a hurry going nowhere
Dropping all my pearls behind
Misplacing all my emeralds
Carrying my own wheat just enough to get by

A NO VACANCY SIGN

I have no place to put today with the last one still hanging around
Looking for a room to lie and rest with all my yesterdays
There's a no vacancy sign in front of my overcrowded mind
With all of my yesterdays piling up on one another
Popping in and out, I just push it aside
And search up in the sky for a star to chart my way

Anthony Cardelli

FATHER TIME

I keep going back to where I left off
I keep going back to the same place
My sense of direction takes the lead just for so long
Then gets mixed up in a traffic jam

So here I am up to now
Stuck in the middle of an overcrowded mind
With a No Vacancy sign
Staring me right in the eye
So I keep turning back to where I left off
And start all over again

If you could spare a minute Father Time
And stop what you're doing
I would like to tell the world before we start again

Let's leave behind all the silver and gold
And carry the seeds to plant the wheat
To give us strength to dig for coal

Let's leave behind all precious metals
And carry the stone to build a foundation,
On emeralds, pearls, and wheat
A house with elegance, depth and strength
Filling each room with Love
The recipe for a home

Let's start the world again
A world you can call your home
A world without limits

A Man of Many Dreams

FORTHCOMING SEASONS

I never put the blame on Mame
Or Mrs. O'Leary's cow
That's the way I've always been
And nothing can change me now
Even Father Time, although he was unkind

I don't want to be unkind to anyone
Especially you, but I feel I am
And the longer I stay here
The more unkind I'll be

I want to go someplace
Where I don't have to communicate
Unless I want to
I want to be alone
Among strangers with familiar faces

My needs, I can cut back to the basics
Three meals a day and take the time,
The full eight hours of rest

I want to vacate my overcrowded mind
And fill it with words of reason
For the forthcoming seasons

Anthony Cardelli

GEMINI

What's the matter Gemini?
I see tears dropping back inside, way down deep
In the place where it's just you and the pain,
The smile on your face

What's the matter Gemini?
There's a smile on your face
But it doesn't fool me
I know it's just a disguise to fool shallow eyes

For behind that smile, I see teardrops falling back
Falling back inside, on the pain I see in your eyes
Don't ask me how I know,
'Cause I once felt the same

A Man of Many Dreams

HALF PAST MY LIFETIME

It's half past my lifetime
With more or less then fifty to go
What you see before you is all I have to show

The past is gone
The present is going
And as far as the future is concerned,
Now that I've reached the point of no return
I know all to well what energy I have left to burn
Only time will tell

(May 31, 1979)

Anthony Cardelli

In My Silence

In my silence
I'm thinking memories that brought me up to here
Memories I carried light and heavy through all these years
The negatives have all gone with the wind
But the positives are in place deep within the darkroom of my mind
I can develop positive prints that never caught the camera's eye
Photographs of the beauty I let slip by

Footprints I Lost in the Sand

I'm looking for footprints I lost in the sand
The footprints I began to follow before I became a man
It was so long ago, I don't even remember the day
But somewhere along the way I went astray
Now it's half past my lifetime
And as I look back, nothing is visible when I walked on the land

A Man of Many Dreams

MEETING WITH MYSELF

I called a meeting with myself
And read the minutes of the last fifty years
Before I was halfway through, I broke down in tears
I couldn't believe what I know was true
All the beauty I let slip through my shallow eyes

POSITIVE PRINTS

When I reached the age of fifty,
I felt inside all the beauty I touched in the past
Negatives that never caught the camera's eye,
Developed from the darkroom of my mind
Positive prints flashed across the sky,
All the beauty I touched to be enjoyed forever
To be seen by no one but me

MY BOW

I'm strumming a different tune
And strings I never used that were tied to my bow
I don't know why in all this time I never bothered to use
Only one picking one finger all day
By the sound of all these strings
I've been missing the music of my life
But from now on not one note will go untouched

Anthony Cardelli

My Favorite Window

When I look in a mirror,
I don't feel the same as I do when I look out the window
I can look out any window
A window with just a wall in view
But as my eyes search,
I feel the joy of Easter on Fifth Avenue

Whenever I feel sad, ugly, and bad,
I go to my favorite window
And look out to feel the beauty pouring into My Soul

My Imagination

When I was a boy,
Imagination ran away with me to faraway places
Speaking the native tongue among the many races
Imagination was running with me,
When I was too young to go to war
Too old to play kick the can

Intelligence came along for the ride
To guide me through the false reality imagination was taking me to
But I was lost in a world no one knew what was coming to
And went along with the crowd to a place where there's no tomorrow
Intelligence wouldn't stand for that attitude and kept on going
Leaving me and my imagination

Yes, somewhere along the way imagination got the best of me
And intelligence passed me in the stretch

A Man of Many Dreams

MY LIFE'S AN OPEN BOOK

My life's an open book
Filled with empty pages for all ages to read
Nothing really happened to me
I'm just one of the billions of beings
Who started out even with a grain of salt
Gaining each day from the faults I made along the way

I never lost a thing in my life
I keep it all in my memories
With the negatives in the darkroom of my mind
Developing photographs in front of me
Of the beauty I left behind

People call me a loser
But that is not how I feel
Because I keep everything in my memory
They only see what I lost on the outside
But their eyes are too shallow to see all I have inside of me

My life's an open book of empty pages
A book without a single word to say
For what ever I did was done before
I've been through love and war
Happiness and despair
I like my steak cooked medium
But the chef keeps serving it rare

Anthony Cardelli

NO MORE

No more dreams, no more fantasies
No more living in a false reality
No more sitting on my hands
Hoping someone will come along

Now is the time to make my stand
No more just along for the ride
No more just one of the boys in the band
I'm through with following and stepping aside

Now is the time to take the lead
With pride shining through my eyes
Feeling the search close to My Heart
Burning the flame in My Soul

SHOULD HAVE

I didn't roll with the punches to soften the blows
I didn't do a damn thing I was told
I went in like a lion and came out like a lamb
I know that doesn't rhyme but who cares
I've got lots of time
So, I'll take it from the top with the change of a few lines

I should have rolled with the punches to soften the blows
I should have bobbed and weaved
Did a sidestep or two
Jabbing with the right
Hooking with the left

A Man of Many Dreams

BEEN HERE ONCE BEFORE

This is the moment I've been waiting for
I always knew someday Mr. Opportunity,
Would knock on my door
It was all uphill since the day I was born
And now that I've reached the summit of my dreams
Strange as it all may seem, somehow I get the feeling
I've been here once before

THE STAR OF MY FAULTS

When I was young
My past was green
My future unforeseen
And threw away each day in between

I'm older now with a past
Longer than the first act of *Hamlet*
A future of short subjects
And dragging scenes in between

I'm not one to put the blame on Mame
Or Mrs. O'Leary's cow
Or the boys in the back room
Of McCloskey's Bar
I wrote the script with words and music
Produced and directed
Featuring myself as
The "Star of My Faults" in life

Anthony Cardelli

THIS GEMINI

Some say I'm sentimental
Others say I'm too temperamental
But then there are those who say
I'm the perfect gentleman

Some say I'm subject to change
From a Jekyll to a Hyde
And during the time in between,
I'm a crazy, mixed-up chap
Ready to apologize for the other guy

If you haven't guessed my sign by now,
You can see "My Star"
It's out mostly every night
Shining brightly in the sky
Watching over This Gemini

A Man of Many Dreams

THIS IS THE LAST TIME

This is the last time
I'm telling it like it is
After this that's all she wrote
I'm packing it in
I'm through with living in sin
I'm changing my style
Washing my hands with a bottle of water,
Shipped from the Nile
Wipe the frown from my face
And start each day with a smile
No more worries no more stress
I'm bringing out the best in me
Something I kept hidden for too long

TWINS OF A GEMINI

Although she has a double
People say they can't tell them apart
As for me, I have no trouble
Even if she's with or without her look-alike
Wearing the same clothes

And when they smile, that's when they separate
The world keeps spinning
And I keep missing my turn around
But one day, I'm going to catch the ring
And settle down

Anthony Cardelli

UNTIL

Up until now
I never thought too much about anything
I never met anything head on
I would just roll with the punches to soften the blows
My favorite song was "Anything Goes"
I would never let anyone come close to where it hurt the most
Way down deep inside
Hiding on the dark side of the sun

WHAT'S THE MATTER, GEMINI

What's the matter Gemini?
What's with the sad-looking face?
Where's the other guy
The one who always breaks up the place

Tell me the story of how in just a short while,
You can change from a Jekyll to a Hyde
From a smile to a frown
What shot you down?
From that high flying cloud you've been sailing on

A Man of Many Dreams

THIS TIME AROUND

This time around
I won't take any chances
I'll take advantage of all the mistakes I made in the past
I blamed it all on my youth and whatever was left over
I'll put the blame on Mame and Mrs. O'Leary's cow

I never wanted to be the featured star
I even went as far as the back room of Mr. Closkey's Bar,
To take my stand behind the boys in the band

This time around
I'm going to make my stand
I'm not going to sit on my hands

This time around
I'm not going to be counted out
Never again will I be one of the boys in the band,
Standing in line waiting for my turn

This time around
I'll give as much as before
But before I get my fingers burned, I'll take a little more
This time around
It's going to be easy
There are no more mistakes to make
I've run out of names on who to blame

Anthony Cardelli

This time around
I know I'll never be the same
For I feel it through my new pair of eyes
All the beauty I missed surrounds me now
And deep within I feel everlasting joy
A place my shallow eyes never felt before

This time around
Let's do it for the beauty
As the world turns on a new day
Let's rise with the sun and follow it every which way,
As it shines on the beauty we missed,
When our eyes were too shallow to feel how deep beauty runs

'Cause this time around all the beauty that surrounds me now
Is beautiful in more ways than one!

A Man of Many Dreams

MYSELF AND I

I talk to myself quite often now
It used to be once in a while way back then
But now it's my only hidden habit
The rest of my habits are out in the open
With no place to go with yesterday in their way,
To a better tomorrow

Myself and I are the same guy
We both feel the same inside
But one of us kept something hidden out there
It was right in front of my eyes

Without the feeling, the feeling inside
There's nothing out there I can get next to
It can be right in front of my eyes
So close and yet so far
Without the feeling
I can't get next to where you are

MY ECHO, MY SHADOW, AND ME

I'm living as gracefully as I can
I've knocked down all the hindering blocks
That were turning my heart into stone
I have accepted for the rest of my life, living alone
The only time I'm lonely is when I'm in the middle of a crowd
Someday I'll find a place to dock
Getting along with me, myself, and I
'Cause we three were not alone
We need no company
My echo, my shadow, and me

Anthony Cardelli

BLACK E BLUE

Cold empty bed springs
Hard as lead
Pains in my head
I feel like Old Ned
What did I do to be so black e blue?

There's no joy for me, no company
Even a mouse runs from my house
All my life through I've been so black and blue

Now, I'm not wise, but deep down inside
I just can't hide the way I feel inside
The way I feel I can't reveal,
The pain inside my head
I'm so alone
My heart is gone

HOPE AND ENCOURAGEMENT

Anthony Cardelli

It's Half Past a Lifetime

I occupy most of my time alone in my thoughts
Talking to myself and really listening in what I'm saying
Sort of a silent game I'm playing

There's no one there to ask,
Who, what, where, when, and why
But me to answer for the character I build inside
It's half past a lifetime
After a decade and two score have gone by
With sad and happy tears, I kiss away those wonderful years

With all the youth in you to throw away
And hurry worry out of your tears
To step into your dreams and fantasies

Yes, it's half past a lifetime
And now, I can see a new life ahead, as clear as can be!
A path never walked on
To lead My Family into the palm,
Of the Daughter of My People's beautiful hands!

A Man of Many Dreams

A New Pair of Eyes

With a new pair of eyes,
I search through the shadows of each day
Speaking words with reason
With a voice well seasoned
People listen and understand along the way
And as my eyes search deeper into the day,
They all agree and believe everything I had to say

I Relish the Moment

I relish the moment, the moment I open my eyes
Feeling the warmth of being alive to begin a new day
Taking it any way it comes with or without the sun
Excepting the gift of life
Once more eager to enjoy the trip
To its journey's end

Leave the Past Behind

Out of sight out of mind
Is a place you'll never find, carrying a heavy past
Take it from me, I've been traveling a little longer than you
The load on my back is beginning to drag me down
So, take it for what it's worth,
If you leave the past behind and don't look back,
Just around the corner you will find a place,
Called out of sight, out of mind

Anthony Cardelli

FREE AS A BIRD

You can count yourself out
Count yourself in
When you're free as a bird,
You can fly where no one has been
You can follow the sun
Or stay behind
Or take the lead
If you had a mind to,
There would be nothing you couldn't do

BETTER TIMES AHEAD

I see better times ahead
With better thoughts in the minds of men
Starting from the first line to the last
The way it was written in the past

All are equal to share in the gift of life
A world full of food and drink
With physical power and understanding minds
With kindness and tender loving care
All are equal to share

THE NEW PRESIDENT

The new President is rolling up his sleeves
And laying down the track to new trails
We wheeled and dealed
Then cut the cards and built a new stack
I think it's time we use some old logs
And lay down the track to new trails
Let bombs come what may
And miss us where we sat

A Man of Many Dreams

Don't Make Waves

We're all going to die sooner or later
We're all in the same boat
So why make waves
There's more than enough fish heads and rice to go around
Think back to what the Man on the mound did with a loaf of bread
Why do we keep forgetting the words He said?

Think of a Happy Time

Whenever I'm sad and lonely before a tear is shed,
I close my eyes to stop the flow and think of a happy time in my life,
To feel within me the joy of beauty
Then my eyes open from the happy tears,
Cascading in the harbor of my life,
Sailing me away from the dim lights casting shadows over the bay

Give It Your Best

Every morning rain or shine
Another day on borrowed time
What to do with this loan is up to you alone
You only get one life to live
And if you're made of the right stuff,
Then once is enough

So give it your best shot
Before you fall down,
From this one time around
You're only here for a visit
Not a permanent guest
Whether your lease in life is long or short,
Give it your best!

Anthony Cardelli

GREAT TO BE ALIVE

There are over a million things in life,
To make you feel great to be alive
Just to mention a few
Because the last thing I want to do is bore you

After a long hot Summer
Doesn't it feel great to inhale a breath of fresh air?
From the leaves falling down
Laying a blanket gently on the ground
Isn't it great to cuddle in December?
Lying in slumber by an open fire
As Mother Nature mixes the colors of the three seasons passed
Into Winter white

KEEP TRYING

No matter how many times you try
Keep trying
If you stop before you reach the top
You'll never see the other side
You'll spend the rest of your life,
Sitting on your hands
Watching everything passing by
You have to make it happen
You can't sit and wait
To inherit the merits you never earned

A Man of Many Dreams

FIRST IMPRESSION

You never get a second chance to make a good first impression
You'd be just wasting precious time to make it your one obsession
You'd be standing around watching things happen,
Instead of making them happen
So don't be unkind to yourself
Don't let time change early in your life
Stick to your natural roots

HEARTBREAK AFFAIR

You just ended a rough and tough love affair. Why it lasted as long as it did, only you can answer. After the blind times of candlelight and wine, you were hit with words below the heart, but like the fighter that you are, you rolled with the punches to soften the blows. You bobbed and weaved to avoid a bloody nose. No matter how you tried, the words kept coming on strong. But you hung in there and went the distance of another heartbreak affair. Now it's time to get your life back. Call up your friends, leave your lovers behind, and put them on hold. Give yourself some space. You don't have to go to Timbuktu. What you need is just around the corner in your mind. Start having the fun you missed, dining and dancing, laughing and singing. The "city that never sleeps" and the "city of brotherly love" are to the left of you and the right of you. When you chase all the demons and you really get back the life you love, growing with your offsprings and friends who love you, you'll realize that happiness makes up in life what it lacks in length.

Anthony Cardelli

IT'S NOT OVER 'TIL IT'S OVER

It's not over 'til it's over
Even when you feel you haven't the slightest chance
I've seen it happen so many times to people just like me and you
Skies turning gray
Dark clouds rolling in
All efforts were in vain

But just when you're about to call the game on account of rain,
The sun suddenly appears, bursting through the clouds!
Spreading beautiful rainbow towels all over the sky
To soak up all over the pain inside
And drying the Sad Tears that welled in our eyes

It's not over 'til it's over
Because sometimes the sun shines when it rains!

A Man of Many Dreams

LET YOURSELF GO

Let yourself go
Take the word of someone who knows
You only live once
But once is enough if you get it right

So stop wasting precious time sitting on your hands
Big Ben never stops; he keeps ticking away

So, may I remind you with these words from a song of the past
"I'm gonna live until I die"!
So give it a try and die happy

LIFE IS BEAUTIFUL

Life is beautiful
In more ways than one
From the beginning of first light
Rising through the darkness of the night

Life follows the sun every which way
With its rays spreading across the sky to new horizons
And when day is done it runs into twilight
A beautiful time to pause and rest,
Under the setting of the sun
Waiting for the moon to appear
For each beam to light up all the stars
To chart life's way through the darkness of the night

Anthony Cardelli

My Special Star

I feel what I see as my eyes search up in the sky,
Beyond my time and place
There's a special star falling through space a million light years away
It began its vast journey since the beginning of time to shine on me
It's half past my lifetime with the clock still running
I keep the faith locked in my heart,
That my special star will enter the atmosphere in time before I depart

Somewhere in Time

Somewhere in time
There's a place just waiting for me to find
I know it's there, I feel it in my bones
It stands high on a hill surrounded with trees
Rich with fruit and leaves
Filled with Love inside
The recipe for a Home

Now Is the Time

Now is the time
To make all of Our Dreams come true
Now is the time
To stop what we're doing
And search with our eyes
And listen to those sounding voices from Paradise!

A Man of Many Dreams

ILLUSIONS OF GRANDEUR

I wished for the moon and did not get it
I took a crack at the stars; forget it
I've come to the conclusion I must be having illusions of grandeur
To think I can make a score by just wishing for

So let mè give you a piece of advice
If you want something in life, wishing won't do it
Sitting on your hands with your knees knocking
Stand up like Rocky and Fight! Fight! Fight!

SHE OPENS MY EYES

This piece of dirt I'm standing on is just a speck to step on
But here I am holding on, hanging in there
Keeping my head above water
Breathing in all I can take
Because it's a miracle every time dawn breaks
She opens my eyes

Every time dawn breaks she opens my eyes
Opens them wide as can be
I could be talking with the crowd
Then dawn breaks into the room
And all the talking settles down to a soft whisper
Toning through the air

Anthony Cardelli

RELISH THE MOMENT

Relish the moment this is the day the Lord hath made
Rejoice and be glad in it
It isn't the burdens of today that drive men mad
It is the regrets over yesterday and the fear of tomorrow
Regrets and fear are twin thieves who rob us of today

So, stop pacing the aisles and counting the miles
Instead, climb more mountains, eat more ice cream
Go barefoot more often, swim more rivers
Watch more sunsets, laugh more, cry less
Life must be lived as we go along
The stations will come soon enough

Stop putting things off that you can enjoy this day, this week, or this year
One of these days, maybe none of these days
There is no station, no place to arrive
The true joy of life is the trip
The station is only a dream
It constantly outdistances us

A Man of Many Dreams

SINCE HEAVEN KNOWS WHEN

Since heaven knows when
That's how long it's been
I kept inside what has taken you a split second to bring out in the open

I haven't seen her since heaven knows when
Between heaven and me,
No one, old friends and new, only see what I allowed
That is, up until now

Hidden emotions are coming out of hiding
Emotions I've kept inside of me, up until now
I'm beginning to reveal exactly how I feel
Whether it hurts or not

Now that I've started, I'm never going to stop
For I have reached an age of immunity to pain
And only feel relief since I've released my emotions to stay in motion
Devoting My Life to you!

Anthony Cardelli

SOMETIMES THE SUN SHINES WHEN IT RAINS

Sometimes the sun shines when it rains
Just when you feel the end is near
It suddenly appears bursting through the clouds
Drying all the tears with beautiful rainbow towels

Sometimes the sun shines when it rains
Just when you feel there's no chance at all
When you're in the bottom of the win and last column
Late in mid season, find yourself
On Top in the fall!

THANKFUL

Up until now, I never saw the sun rise
It was always described through other eyes
That is, up until now
For now I feel the sun rising in me,
From the smile on your face
I feel its warmth knowing you are near, without an embrace
And from the sound of your voice, I sense love at first sight
And I thank God for letting me see you tonight

A Man of Many Dreams

The Postman

The postman always rings twice for those who miss their calling in life.

They spend the rest of their time sitting on their hands hoping he will ring again. Someone once said the saddest words from tongue or pen, the saddest are these, "What might have been." No matter what it maybe, if you believe your good enough to do it, go after it, keeping in mind that talent is the least important thing a person needs, but humility is the one thing he must have. You pay your dues beginning from the bottom to the top. Once you get there you can't sit down and enjoy the view you still owe a good performance to the people you once knew. You'll know when you've paid up, for there will come a night there'll be no boos. There'll only be the roar of the crowd and smell of the grease paint, jammed with a taste of honey. Standing up front pleasantly proud of doing the right thing, in the right place, at the right time. With that Piccolo feeling of 100 percent body and mind with the right people.

Anthony Cardelli

WHAT'S THE MATTER, FRIEND?

What's the matter, friend?
There's a teardrop in your eye
Come laugh like me
'Tis only babes and women that should cry

But if you can't hold back the tears,
That has been filling up to the wall you build inside
Then break down in style
Crack into a smile and let it all out
That's part of what life is all about!

WITH OR WITHOUT THE SUN

I knew it wouldn't be easy
But I never thought it would be this hard
I kept telling myself this too shall pass
But why do I have this everlasting feeling,
The worst has yet to come

Someone once said the only thing permanent is change
But as the world turns on another new day,
With or without the sun my life is the same
So, I take each day as it comes
With or without the sun

A Man of Many Dreams

WHERE THERE'S A WILL

Where there's a will,
There's a way, they say
Remember, Rome wasn't built in a day
But it sure feels good when it comes out right
No matter how many times you try
When it comes out right,
It makes all the other times worthwhile

You can be at the bottom of the win
And last column in midseason
With reason thinking no chance at all
When all of a sudden you get it altogether
And wind up on Top in the fall

So, don't count yourself out before the game is over
The next second is time enough to make your play
For where there's a will, there's a way!

Anthony Cardelli

LIFE AFTER DEATH

I saw a Light as I was passing through the dark side of the moon
There, standing in a garden,
Surrounded with fresh scented flowers in full bloom,
Was a beautiful lady dressed in white

With open arms she welcomed me into Eternal Life
Even though she knew in all the time I lived on earth,
I doubted the words of my mother to be true

And as I entered there standing behind her,
Smiling with happy tears, was my father,
Once a non-believer too,
Told me that the words of my mother are true
Now we both are waiting for you!

A Man of Many Dreams

THERE WILL COME A TIME

There will come a time in your life
When you'll stop the clock and pause to step aside
To let the past pass by
And take a good look until it catches up . . . up until now
And pick up all the "Pearls" you dropped,
When your eyes were too shallow to feel how deep they fell,
 Into the well of the whirlpool you dwelled in

There will come a time in your life
When you'll find yourself back to square one
Back to where you started from
A Heart full of broken dreams
With empty pockets running down the seams
Picking up where you left off
Building your Rome in one day
With only the stars to chart your way
Weathering through the storm
Bending to knee level winds around The Horn

Yes, there will come a day
When nature will change your course
To the calm of the summer palm
Swaying through the branches of Your Family Tree!

FAREWELLS

A Man of Many Dreams

A HEAVY TOLL

I may go sooner than expected
And I would like to say,
Life with you has been beautiful in every way
These are not just words coming out of my head
But from my heart and soul
For life without you would have made my death,
A heavy toll

BEFORE YOU GO

Before you go
Take My Love with you
Because without you it would be to heavy to carry
I would never be able to make it on my own
With so much to give,
With such a heavy load,
With no place to empty

Anthony Cardelli

WHEN I DIE

When I die
Bury me among the ancient dead
Lay me down to rest on a grassy hill lock
Surrounded with trees
Rich with fruit and leaves
Shutting out the sun
With its rays slipping through the branches

UNTIL THE DAY I DIE

From the corner of my eye
I caught a glimpse of beauty passing by
But when I turned to get a better view,
You were nowhere in sight
Leaving me standing there with just a glimpse
Of the beauty I will feel inside,
Until the day I die

A Man of Many Dreams

DEAR FRIENDS

Here's to old times, Dear Friends
To precious time that will never tick again
Only in our hearts it skips a beat
Now and then, when we think of when,
We were buddies to the end

To the best of times, the worst of times
We mixed the good with the bad
And came up with a recipe, each one of us
But in our hearts each precious moment of its memories,
Silently skips a beat

HERE'S LOOKING AT YOU

Here's looking at you, kid
May time be as kind the next time we meet,
In-between now and when
I'll carry with me this moment in a special place
In the darkroom of my mind
To light my way to the time we meet again

Anthony Cardelli

REST HIS SOUL

God please rest his soul
He carried a heavy load all the while he was on earth
He kept the flame up high
To burn all the love he poured into its hearth

God, please rest his soul
Let him lie in your love
For he left all his love behind to the ones who remain
To bare the pain from the loss of his body
But bare in mind the beautiful memories gained!

TAKE THE TIME

Before we go our separate ways,
I always say good-bye each day
Just in case I leave this place,
My love will know I took the time to say good-bye

TEARS

If you're going to say good-bye,
Say it without tears
Save the tears until we meet again
Keep them hidden from the sun
For when that day comes,
The tears that will fall will be happy ones

A Man of Many Dreams

TOUCHED IN TIME

We touched in time what more can we ask for
We met on the level and poured out all we had to share
For we both knew somewhere in time we would part on the square

Now that you're leaving,
The cross I have to bare will be light to carry
For my shoulders will never feel the strain,
Of the precious cargo I'll carry

TRAIL OF TEARS

The trail of tears I left behind are running over the falls of sorrow
Mixed with sadness and despair
In a whirlpool of hatred beyond compare

May the trail of tears I leave behind,
Be happy ones to drown all the sorrows yet to come,
For My Loved Ones to follow

Anthony Cardelli

WITH THIS KISS

With this kiss,
I blow into the wind
To be carried to places we have never been
And if by chance we part
And go our separate ways,
This kiss will be yours
To taste the flavors of Our Love,
In some distant place

ETERNAL LOVE

The day I leave, I'll take with me all the Love you gave me
And leave behind all the Love I had to give
With Your Love I'll be able to rest
Knowing you will find when it's your time,
The nest of Our Family Tree
Bringing back to me the Love I left behind
Eternal Love, yours and mine!

EPILOGUE

A New World

Eighty-two years have past
The wealth in my dreams has come true
In-between all the mistakes along the wrong turns I made
I turned to the right one hundred and eighty degrees
I feel I discovered a New World
Being given the gift of witnessing the fourth generation,
Adding to my family tree
I'm not going to sit on my hands and hope
I'm entering into this New World as a Professional
The Amateur I'm leaving behind

Antonio
June 21, 2011

Anthony Cardelli

My Fourth String

Put-tin the past on hold
Put-tin all my energy into the present
I'm not giving up on the future
Beyond it, is the mystery
As of today, June 21, 2011, the future is tomorrow
I feel something new is ahead of me
Something I've been doing all my life
The fourth string tied to my bow
Writing

To be continued . . .

July 19, 2014